Online Customers!

A "How To" Guide for Phoenix Business Owners

By

Marlene Allen
and
Valerie Dawson

Copyright © 2014

ISBN-13:
978-1494797171

ISBN-10:
1494797178

Published in the United States of America

All Rights Reserved

All rights reserved. No part of this book may be reproduced or transmitted in any form or by any means, electronic or mechanical, including photocopying, recording or by any information storage and retrieval system, without written permission from the authors, except for the inclusion of brief quotations in a review.

Limit of Liability Disclaimer: The information contained in this book is for information purposes only, and may not apply to your situation. The author, publisher, distributor and provider provide no warranty about the content or accuracy of content enclosed. Information provided is subjective. Keep this in mind when reviewing this guide.

Neither the Publisher nor Authors shall be liable for any loss of profit or any other commercial damages resulting from use of this guide. All links are for information purposes only and are not warranted for content, accuracy, or any other implied or explicit purpose.

Earnings Disclaimer: All income examples in this book are just that – examples. They are not intended to represent or guarantee that everyone will achieve the same results. You understand that each individual's success will be determined by his or her desire, dedication, background, effort and motivation to work. There is no guarantee you will duplicate any of the results stated here. You recognize any business endeavor has inherent risk for loss of capital.   "The typical result one can expect to achieve is nothing. The "typical" person never gets to the end of this book. The "typical" person fails to implement anything. Thus they earn nothing. Zero. No income. And perhaps a loss of income. That's because "typical" people do nothing and therefore they achieve nothing. Be atypical. Do something. Implement something. If it doesn't work; Try again.

TABLE OF CONTENTS

1	How To Use The Internet To Fill Your Business	5
2	How to Get New Customers the RIGHT Way Online	19
3	How to Choose Keywords to Promote Your Business	41
4	Blogging and Advanced Local Search Techniques	59
5	Using Facebook, LinkedIn, and Other Platforms	75
6	How to Use Directories to Get More Customers	99
7	How To Use Online Reviews to Drive Your Marketing	113
8	Using Automation	131
9	ROI and Making More Than You're Spending	139
10	Where Do I Go From Here	149
11	How To Get All of This Done	165

INTRODUCTION

Why a book about the Internet for Phoenix Business Owners

At first, it didn't make sense. The Internet changes every day, and once it's printed, the book will be around forever.

Then, we realized that while the Internet is constantly changing, there are tried and true principles that will never change. In fact, they will only increase in effectiveness as the Internet grows and traditional advertising fades away.

In this book you will find the best of both worlds.

Inside are constant principles. In other words, they work...when you implement them. They are based on the same solid strategies that we have been using with our clients in Phoenix and the surrounding area for years.

The results speak for themselves.

On that note, the difference between average businesses and *great* businesses comes down to implementation. One often differs from another only in their willingness to implement the things they learn.

The same is true for the information in this book. It works, and similar to everything you learned in school, it only works when implemented. You *knowing* all of this information won't help you make any more money or sell your services or even your practice for more. When you *implement* it, this information can make you an additional six figures or more in a year, PLUS you will help more people, create a more stable business, and gain some bragging rights at the next business conference you attend.

Use it, then send us your success story!

On that note, one of the most common questions we get from business owners in Phoenix is, "How am I supposed to get all of this done?"

The answer is that smart business owners know how to build (or find) good teams. On that note, toward the end of the book, we have included a section on how to contact our team to help you implement your web strategy.

Ready? Let's get started!

1

HOW TO USE THE INTERNET TO FILL YOUR BUSINESS

Congratulations! Just by getting to this first chapter, you're already ahead of your competition in Phoenix!

Why? Well, most people don't take the necessary action for success. You've gotten this far, now let's go the rest of the way together. At least you're forward-thinking. You know that the Internet is a big deal, and you know that you might use the Internet to drum up business here and there, if you can, and maybe this book can also help you supplement your advertising.

You may think that the Internet won't help you all that much. People know you, you're in the Yellow Pages, advertise n the Newspaper, and you're still getting a healthy amount of business.

Who searches for a local business on the Internet, anyway?

The majority of your potential customers, that's who!

Recent research shows that, increasingly, fulfillment of online searches is done overwhelmingly by local businesses. A 2010 study by BIA/Kelsey and research firm ComStat found that a staggering 97% of consumers research their purchases and local services online before they fulfill them at a local business. This isn't just the case with local services, either; major e-retailers are being beaten out by customers who research products online but choose to buy them at local stores. This seems to speak to the fact that people like human interaction; they inform themselves online, but in the end they want that personal connection. Your business however is not something that can be fulfilled online. Thankfully, you are the connection to the procedure they desire.

The consequence of this is that, unfortunately, any business with no (or substandard) Internet presence is left out of that research process. People want to fulfill their online searches locally, but if you don't pop up when they're doing their research, you'll simply fly under their radar and lose your business to another who has that Internet presence.

This is, of course, potentially very dangerous for any local business owner who has thus far avoided being on the Internet, whose website is not producing results, or has not at least started the process to have a good online presence. It may sound alarmist or like nonsense, but it's true: the majority of your potential customers are looking for their representation on the Internet, even preferring it over more traditional media like the Yellow Pages or TV. In fact, a recent 2009 study by comScore and TMP Directional Marketing showed that, for the first time, the number of customers searching for local businesses on the Internet exceeded that of the Yellow Pages, and Yellow Pages has headed downhill ever since. The fact of the matter is that people simply don't use the Yellow Pages, and other traditional media anymore, since the Internet is a much easier and more convenient way to get information.

It's surprising at first, but it begins to make sense once you think about it. You can even look to your own habits as proof of this changing trend; how often do you use the Yellow Pages or the newspaper, or a magazine to find something you're looking for? Do you run over to your desk and flip through it to find what you need, or do you do a quick Google search and find what you need right away? Even if you're still a traditional media user, take a look at others, your kids, friends, and family. How many of them use the Yellow Pages, a newspaper or a magazine? If you're honest with yourself, it won't be surprising at all that the way people look for services has changed.

What is surprising is how many businesses still have huge portions of their budget devoted to the Yellow Pages and print ads. Many businesses can have $20,000 or more allocated to their print media advertising budget, which is, in this day and age, simply a waste of money; print media simply just isn't returning enough business to justify that sort of major investment. Of businesses that can or do track ROI from print advertising campaigns, virtually all of them have seen diminishing returns. Every month, without fail, more people are using Google and other search engines instead of traditional media and methods of research; this isn't just a passing trend. Search has supplanted print media, and it's here to stay! An effective online presence isn't just a temporary strategy—it's forward-looking towards a future that has search engines as the main tool customers use to make their decisions.

What that means for you

First, let's get one thing for certain: The sooner you get an online presence the better. If you don't get moving soon, it will require more work as time goes on to catch up with your competition.

Another interesting fact: An online presence is considered

equity in a business. It is worth a great deal when you go to sell your practice. Whether you like it or not, It is a necessary part of doing business, and your ultimate goal of eventually selling your business.

So how do you get in on this search corner of the market? After all, don't big businesses dominate search engine rankings on the Internet? Can local businesses even compete in this ferocious online arena?

As it turns out, they can. Google has made some of the most significant changes to their search algorithm that we've seen in a long time; specifically, they've shifted searches for brick & mortar businesses to something called "local search return" or specifically Google Places / Google + Local, a feature that used to be only available on their Google Maps service.

What is local search return? Originally, when a user searched on Google Maps, local businesses would pop up in the area the user was searching for. If a user searched "New York, NY", for example, the Google interactive map that would appear also had helpful markers placed around the map, indicating local businesses that were nearby. Restaurants and hotels were the first businesses to jump on this feature and utilize it, and it was a natural fit; visitors to a new city need to know places to eat and sleep, and the Google Maps local search return feature was very useful to both users and customers by showing users where these local businesses were and facilitating that offline conversion.

Very soon, however, businesses besides restaurants and hotels realized that this service could benefit them greatly, and began listing themselves on the local search return maps as well. Eventually, Google realized that if users were searching maps to get this kind of information, then probably many of them are also searching in the regular search text box as well, not realizing that they had to go to the maps section to get those local search results. Again, look at your own search habits; how often do you go to Google Maps to search for something? Most likely, you simply type it into the google.com search box and hit enter.

Now, at this point in time, Google's regular search box was just returning lists of links as search results; they weren't map-based and often weren't nearly as useful as the map results that Google Maps was returning. As a result, Google started incorporating the local search returns into their regular search page. When you search for a brick & mortar business now on Google, it returns a map as well, with up to seven marked locations on the map that are all local businesses. This is great news for local businesses, because now there's a real chance for competition: a year ago, or even six months ago, local businesses simply couldn't compete on a national level with giants like Amazon or Wikipedia. Now, however, there's a very real chance for your business to show up in the top three results on a local search page, a chance that will undoubtedly boost your offline conversion, and a chance that wasn't there even a year ago.

landscapes

Web Images Maps Shopping More ▾ Search tools

About 34,600,000 results (0.24 seconds)

Landscape Photos - National Geographic
photography.nationalgeographic.com/photography/photo.../landscapes/ ▾
Photos of **landscapes** around the world, including deserts, mountains, seascapes, forests, valleys, and more from National Geographic.
Photos - Night Sky - Patagonia - Horses, Iceland - Provins, France

Landscape - Wikipedia, the free encyclopedia
en.wikipedia.org/wiki/Landscape ▾
Landscape comprises the visible features of an area of land, including the physical elements of landforms such as (ice-capped) mountains, hills, water bodies ...

Landscape art - Wikipedia, the free encyclopedia
en.wikipedia.org/wiki/Landscape_art ▾
The word "**landscape**" entered the modern English language as landskip (variously spelt), an anglicization of the Dutch landschap, around the start of the 17th ...

Images for **landscapes** - Report images

The Luminous **Landscape**
www.luminous-landscape.com/ ▾
The web's most comprehensive site devoted to the art of **landscape** and nature photography using traditional as well as digital image processing techniques.

 landscapes scottsdale az

Web Images Maps Shopping More ▾ Search tools

About 2,750,000 results (0.37 seconds)

Desert Environments **Landscape** and Design
landscapedesignersaz.com
Google+ page

Sonoran Rain **Landscape** Creations, LLC
www.sonoranrain.com
Google+ page

DCL Inc
plus.google.com
Google+ page

Harper's Nurseries and **Landscape** Co.
www.harpersnurseries.com
3 Google reviews

Arte Verde
www.arteverde.com
Google+ page

Sara Jacoby **Landscape** Design, LLC
www.sarajacoby.com
3 Google reviews

A & A Materials Inc
www.aamaterialsinc.com
Google+ page

(A) Scottsdale
(408) 708-3177

(B) 8087 E Lariat Ln
Scottsdale
(480) 502-5344

(C) 15030 N 53rd St
Scottsdale
(602) 996-1229

(D) 2529 N Hayden Rd
Scottsdale
(480) 946-3481

(E) 8300 N Hayden Rd #207
Scottsdale
(480) 367-9337

(F) 8637 E Sandalwood Dr
Scottsdale
(480) 293-4163

(G) 10333 E McDowell Rd
Scottsdale
(480) 990-0557

See results for **landscapes scottsdale az** on a map »

The screenshot of "landscapes Scottsdale AZ" here should prove how powerful that local search return feature is. Before, you had no chance of competing in any search; now, local businesses have a chance to come out on top for local searches in their area. True, it's not easy; there are plenty of other businesses vying for these same spots, and just having a website up and some keywords isn't going to get you anywhere (and in fact, doing this process poorly can ensure that you never see the front page of Google at all). There is a process, however, and if you do a good job, are careful, and follow all the instructions in this book you'll have a very good shot at hitting the A, B, or C spots on your local search return!

NOTE:

We mentioned that Google has changed its search algorithm- one of those changes involves duplicate content, which is now more dangerous than ever! Google has said many times, both verbally and in print that it is striving to reward the real local business that has quality and substance to offer to their community. As a result, they are cracking down very harshly on anyone who's trying to game the system with shady methods such as duplicate content or fake listings; such actions will get you delisted from Google's search index entirely, and possibly for good. Though this may seem harsh or unreasonable, remember that Google's efforts to clean up its search engine only benefits you; you want them to go after the scammers and spammers so that you, a real business who can offer value and quality to consumers, can rise to the top to people who are genuinely looking for help and services.

In a similar vein, be very, very wary of companies who tell you this process is easy! <u>It's not</u>. They'll tell you it's just a matter of keywords, and to buy content and put it on multiple sites and your own. The problem is, much of this content is almost always rehashed, rewritten, or outright duplicated content, and you'll get next to no credit with Google at best, and delisted at worst. It also cuts two ways, because not only are you not gaining any ground, you're actually losing ground because Google's penalizing you. It's definitely not the way to go, and you'll be falling behind your competitors if you try and take this easy way out.

Quality content has always been the centerpiece for being successful online, and that doesn't show any signs of changing. Creating quality content doesn't have to be hard, but it does take time, patience, and discipline: there's a process to follow to ensure that you have the right kind of quality content that will get you ranked sky-high on Google! People have been trying to game the system with duplicate content and link farms for years, but Google has caught on to this sort of trickery and it's rapidly disappearing from the search engine landscape. Make sure not to get scammed by any of these offers – you know that if it seems too easy or cheap to be true- <u>odds are that it probably is</u>! Ask them if their content is duplicated, rewritten, or appears anywhere else; if they hem and haw before answering, run for the hills and don't look back!

But you haven't gone to those other companies; you bought this book. With it, you've received the system and process you need that will, with some time, effort, patience, and planning, get you to the top of the search results for your area!

SUMMARY:

- <u>The Internet is no longer optional</u>. More and more, people are using it to find businesses and needs: You need to leverage it!

- Search is the big player now in Internet marketing. You need to make sure your page ranks high in the list of results when users search!

- Be very careful of how you enter the search engine market! A substandard presence online can be worse than no presence at all.

- If you need help, make sure to choose your marketers carefully! Some may attempt underhanded tricks to boost you in the search rankings (like duplicate content) but these tricks can often carry with them severe penalty from the search engines for trying to game the system!

2

GET NEW CUSTOMERS THE RIGHT WAY ONLINE

So now that you know how important Google is; as we've taken a look at how recent changes have made local search return, and Google ranking in general, extremely important to your marketing efforts. We know that traditional media is fading away fast, and if you want to stay on top of the game you're going to have to get into this search business fast!

The natural next step would be to get an online presence and to get it ranked, and for that you need a website. Your website is as much a part of this process as anything else, and if you're going to get good conversions from your search rankings you need a functional website that fully caters to both the needs of your business and the needs of your customers.

The creation of the website can be a real eye-opener, especially in today's whiz-bang, Flash-enabled, Web 2.0 world where graphic designers think every website needs interactive menus, drop-down interfaces, and all other sorts of bells and whistles. You see it all the time, in fact, people ask for "Web 2.0" or "interactive" developers, or developers will try to push 'Flash this' or 'Web 2.0 that' on you, saying how important it is and how professional it makes your site look. You may be tempted to believe them. Remember this: You are talking to graphic designers, not internet marketers. There is a BIG Difference.

The truth, however, is this: for most practices and conversion rates, all of that fancy stuff does not matter. A solid, simple website will work far better at increasing your conversion and getting customers to contact you. This may seem counter-intuitive, especially in a world that seems to value style over substance, but it's true: simpler pages have, both in our experience and in the experience of others, are far more effective at getting customers to call or email you than other, fancier, flashier pages.

This will seem a little daunting, especially considering how much we've been talking about the importance of getting listed properly. And that still holds true: getting ranked high on Google still matters the most. In fact, the rest of the book after this chapter is devoted to that very concept. The website, however, is an integral part of the process. It's by no means the most important part in the process, not by far; it's required to be done well, however, or it has the potential to ruin the entire concept of getting ranked on Google. The bottom line is this: if a prospective customer doesn't actually pick up the phone and call, all that effort you put into getting visitors to your site will have been wasted. No matter how flashy, how fancy, how up-to-date your website is, if there are no conversions, then that website is not working for you, plain and simple!

So What Does A Good Website Look Like?

It's a good question: if the flashy, stylish websites aren't for you, what is? What is the secret to getting potential customers to pick up the phone and call?

Well, there are a few things. Let's take a look at them and find out how to build the website that will get the most visitors to pick up that phone and call your business!

Site Construction: What Should Your Overall Site Look Like?

In general, there is a rule that can be applied to websites wishing to get conversions from local search return: The less fancy the website is, the more conversions you'll get from it. Solid, functional sites will be far more effective for you. Keeping that in mind, here is a general outline of what a sample website layout might look like:

- Home page
- Blog
- About Us / Services

- Contact Us (with map and phone)

And that's it.

It might seem a bit *underwhelming* to you, and vastly smaller than the majority of the websites you've visited, and you're right: those websites, however, are not as effective. Your website should be lean and mean, built for one purpose and one purpose only—to get people who go to your website to call you or email you. Anything else is a waste; it's nice that people come to visit your site, but that doesn't mean anything if nobody calls or if you don't capture someone's phone or email for future follow up. Giving too many choices of what they can do on your website is confusing some and a confused mind will take no action.

Every page must also include a call to action. A call to action is something to get visitors to call you or email you right away. We'll talk more about the call to action later in the follow-up section, but just know that for local business websites we recommend, at a minimum, you include a banner or header that appears on every page and make sure your phone number appears in the top-right hand side or middle-right hand side. Studies show, and our experience confirms, that people's eyes gravitate toward the right side of a page -- hint, look where Google puts their ads in their own search results. For an added chance of interaction, add a sign up form beneath the top phone number to sign up for your newsletter or to provide a reason, or an incentive, such as a free report, for people to provide their phone number and email address.

This is, of course, just an example; you are free to modify this layout however you wish. Depending on your business, you may want to add a page about upcoming events you are hosting, or recent news and press about your business. Know, however, that this basic layout works extremely well, and always, always remember: the less fancy the page, the better the results!

NOTE:

Please do not confuse less-fancy with bad design. You still want your business and website to look professional and we advocate a clean simple design. In fact we strongly feel that having less 'flashiness' to a website often leads to better visual design as there is less clutter, and better visual design also helps with conversions. Your business may already have invested in working with a branding agency to help create a logo and a set of colors that represent your "brand", incorporate those into your website. There are a number of color palette tools online where you can enter your logo's main colors and they will provide you with suggested, visually appealing, complementary colors, for example see http://www.colourlovers.com or http://colorcombos.com. It may also be a good time to look at your logo and branding to see if it may be time to update them. The larger businesses are doing that quite frequently.

Look, you are a valuable professional in your community and your services are not (and should not be) cheap – don't make your website give potential clients the wrong impression. This means you may not want to do it yourself and that you should be careful hiring your sister's friend's 22-year-old kid that calls himself a webmaster, but lives in his parents' spare room.

Now, let's go into each of these pages more in-depth!

Home Page

There's not too much individuality going on here, but it's important for this page to connect your reader with the rest of the site. Make sure the page is easy on the eyes, has a blurb about you, and invites the reader to explore more of the site. Above all, however, make absolutely sure that the home page prominently features the blog!

This is so important, I'm going to give it its own line: Make sure the home page prominently features the blog.

There are many ways to do this. Some businesses have the actual blog on the homepage; if you don't want to do this, think very, very carefully about how to prominently integrate your blog with the home page.

Video is another important component for the homepage. Studies have shown a 30% increase in conversions when a visitor can watch a video of someone from the business on the homepage.

<u>Yes, that is 30%</u>!

Incorporate a small, short (90 seconds – 2 minutes maximum) video on your home page.

If you have any copy on your home page, it should only be about no more than 3 things:

1. The benefits you provide someone (not your services or 'features') but the actual benefits clients achieve as a result of working with you.
2. Information about what is on your blog and links or enticements to good blog posts
3. Call to action – what can you provide in exchange for them to call or provide you their email or phone number. Special offers, special reports, checklists, etc.

These 3 items are so important to the success of a website that we actually write these sections for our private clients and place them word-for-word.

Blog

Don't underestimate the blog, it's one of the most vital (if not the most vital) part of your website! It provides two things that are critical to your online success.

First, it is the home to new and relevant content to your prospects and customers. You can talk about a lot of things that will be 'relevant' to them. Obviously, you can discuss interesting things happening that affect your readers within your particular areas of business; if you focus on bookkeeping services, then talk about those services that people are most interested in, etc. You can also link out to a few recent news articles and provide some commentary about how they affect your readers. A hidden gem of relevant content that most practices overlook is to talk about local information. It doesn't have to pertain at all. You are a member of a community and if there is a big marathon, charity find drive, festival, or parade coming up, then write a few paragraphs about that and include links to all the details in one place. If you know that parking is tough on Saturdays around the area, provide information about other parking; if there's a booth at the festival not to be missed, then tell your readers about that. You will be surprised that these will become your most popular blog posts. It also builds up your credibility as someone who lives, works, and cares about your community!

The second thing a blog provides is a place for the search engines to find new and relevant content about what your business does and where it provides those services. Everything we discussed above helps accomplish that, and by talking about your industry or area of practice you will naturally use the keywords that the search engines will pick up. Furthermore, talking about things happening in the local community will help the search engines understand the community, town, or city you should be associated with in the search results. We hope that was simple to understand; very often, many marketers make this part sound more complicated than it has to be. They talk about keywords, keyword density, latent search algorithms, and more. It doesn't have to be that hard! Write about stuff that you know about and that provide value to your readers: the two most obvious are your area and events going on in your community and nearby communities. If you hear someone talk about keyword density, while it's important, just run away: it's our humble opinion that they're just trying to make it sound too complicated so they can charge more.

Over the years, we have learned a lot about working with local businesses. While we know that consistent blogging is important, getting our clients to actually write twice a week in addition to their daily tasks and procedures was like trying to saddle a cow. That's why we made the decision to do all of the writing for our clients. We hired staff writers (good ones who already write as a profession) and paid them well. The results are great. Our clients get good content several times per week...and they don't have to do any of the work!

That's how important blogging is to us!

About Us

The About Us page is, oddly enough, one that many businesses get wrong. They're all too happy just to put up a little blurb about themselves, or about the team, perhaps a map or two on how to get to them. This isn't enough information on you, and nor is it helping you drive conversions. People care about your years of experience sure, but that's not what's going to get them to call- it doesn't truly distinguish you from the other local businesses in the pack, or give them a reason to give <u>you</u> their business. You have to think instead about something called a *unique selling position*- why do clients currently like to work with you and continue working with you? Information about you, your business, why you're different, etc. and so forth just doesn't cut it—you have to <u>show them</u> why you're ahead of the pack, and ultimately show them why they, as a consumer, want to work with you and not the other guy.

Think about it this way: most people care about one thing and one thing only. WIIFM. That stands for "What's In It For Me." Your prospects could honestly care less about your degrees, titles, or positions. Sorry. What they really want to know is if you can solve their problem, and provide the service professionally.

So instead of talking about you, talk about them and what they will benefit from working with you.

That one tip alone, in fact, will set your website above and beyond most of the businesses we see and even some we work with: they simply don't set themselves apart sufficiently, and by doing so you'll gain a very competitive edge in this field.

Contact Us

The Contact Us page should be very simple. You should have your email, your phone number, and a map to your business. That's it. You can perhaps put a slightly different or stronger call to action on this page, but for the most part this page should be clean, simple, and have nothing to distract the reader from picking up the phone or putting in their email. Some people add a contact form on this page. That's perfectly fine to do, but the most important thing is to provide a clear phone number or email that is directed and answered by an actual human.

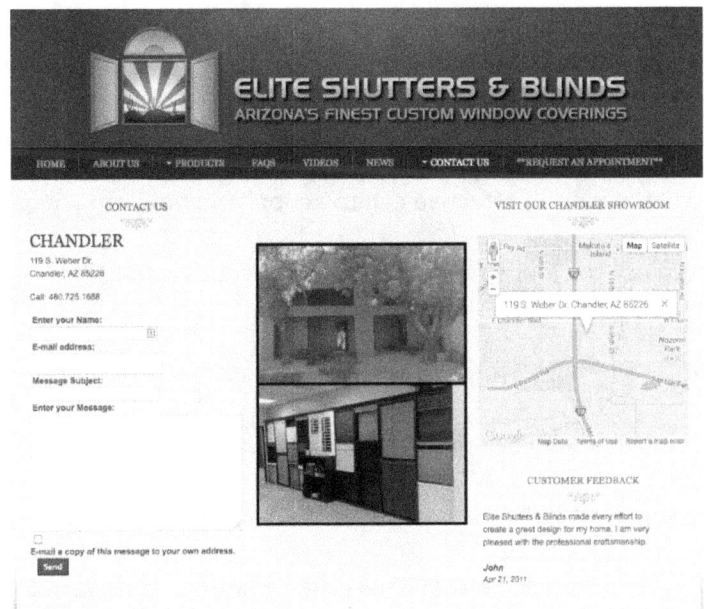

Call To Action

So you've got the basic layout of your page all down. Just one thing left: your call to action (CTA).

So what makes an effective call to action, and how can you put that to use on your site to generate those conversions?

An effective call to action is one that makes the customer pick up the phone and call right away, or give you their email. It's crucial that your call to action is very strong, because you're asking for information that's become something considered more and more private in modern times. People know about spam, they know about scams, and they're hesitant to give out their email to just any site they find on the Internet. You have to overcome that initial hesitation and get them to give you their email. One way is to offer a special for providing information or calling now – like a big discount on a service. However, we've found that the way that works best is to provide a special report about something that will be very helpful to the consumer who found you by searching for a doctor in your area. Examples of this could be "Special Report: 3 Critical Things You Need to

Know Before Calling a Plumber", or "5 Key questions to Ask Your CPA to Make Sure You Don't Overpay on Your Taxes", or "3 Myths You've Been Led to Believe about Financial Investors". It's important that these examples be specific to your business; the more targeted your examples, the more likely it is that you're going to get someone to sign up who's interested in your area of business. You can even make it more targeted by making it local, for example "3 Things You Need to Know Before Selecting a Chiropractor in Phoenix, Arizona". These examples should be strong enough to get someone to put in their email; you want them thinking, "Hey, wow, I was going to look up more chiropractors tomorrow, but I better read about this before I do anything" and then pop in their email. Now you can quickly follow up with them (and even automate some of the follow-up).

This content is so important, that for our private clients, we write this report for them and place it on their website (after their review, of course). The titles above take a "consumer advocacy" approach, which we've found gets a lot more clients than much traditional advertising.

We also typically recommend that you not just ask for their email, but for their cell phone number as well. People are giving out their cell phone numbers quite readily now, more so than a few years ago, where it was very difficult to get someone's mobile number. Many people nowadays use cell phones as their primary or even only phone number, and thus they're more willing to give it out to people who ask if the reason is compelling enough. Google Voice has created a feature that lets you use a different phone number from your own, so that you're not actually giving out your real cell phone number.

If you follow all these steps, anyone who enters in their email or phone number will be a "warm" lead. A "warm" lead is someone who's going to be very receptive to your business and much easier to convert into a client, since they've showed a great deal of interest in your services—they've pretty much done the hard part, which is getting in contact. You have to act on this, however; warm leads, like anything else warm, tend to cool over time, and if you don't act quickly it'll be that much harder to seal the deal. This leads us to our next item of interest: follow-up systems!

It's important that you have some sort of follow-up system in place so that you can call a lead within five minutes of them entering a form on a webpage. It's vital that you have a stable, reliable follow-up system in place! If you can get them within 5 minutes, for example, you know they're an extremely warm lead; you know they were on the website, you know they were interested, and you know they're looking for business! This is a very warm lead, and much more so than someone who just happened to see your name in a direct mail piece or in a local flyer.

There are some automated follow-up systems in place that are used by many businesses; tools like Instant Customer which fully integrates with Constant Contact, and others. Depending on your area of expertise there are some services that even provide dozens of pre-written email templates that have proven to help convert email prospects into clients. If you want to use something like these, that's perfectly fine, but make sure to put the call to action on them first.

We'll talk more about follow-up later, in its own in-depth, complete section. First, in the following chapter however, let's get to the real deal, the heart and soul of this book—before you build that website, let's talk about getting your site noticed and getting it found so the search engines can send people to your site!

SUMMARY:

- Don't lose focus when designing a website: a website is for one purpose and one purpose only, and that's to get people to get in touch with you!

- Fancy is never better: plain is best here! Avoid whiz-bang Flash sites, and get a good designer to make a clean, simple, functional web site to convert leads.

-Blogs are a vital part of a website's success: make yours the home page, or at least featured quite prominently on the home page!

- Following up is absolutely critical: you should have automated systems in place that follow-up with prospective patients the moment they get in touch with you.

3

HOW TO CHOOSE KEYWORDS TO PROMOTE YOUR BUSINESS

Having a website is all well and good, but it doesn't do much for you if nobody visits it. We'll have to get Google to notice you and rank you highly, and we'll do that using targeted keywords. We aren't going to make this a complicated discussion, but it is an important concept to understand.

What are keywords, you ask? Keywords are the words (either one word or multiple words) that users type into Google before they click search. A multiple-word keyword, like "leaky faucet", or "plugged up drain", is called a long-tail keyword phrase. When a user enters one of these keyword phrases, they will get back what Google thinks is most relevant to their search; more specifically, Google returns what it thinks are the best search results for the specific keyword phrase that the user entered in the search box.

That, in a nutshell, is what a keyword is. Our questions, however, are a bit more complicated: What keywords should we use? What keywords will get Google to notice that we're the best search result for a specific keyword phrase?

We have many clients who choose to have us do all of their Internet marketing for them. When we sit down at the table to discuss our plans for their Internet marketing strategies, there are two mistakes we see almost every time when we start talking about keywords:

1) Our new client will be very excited to show us that they're ranking #1 for their particular business name, like "Becky's Bakery". So excited, in fact, that it's almost tough to tell them that that's nothing to be excited about: next to nobody is searching for their exact company name on the Internet. If they

are, it means they already know the company and know what the company does. They've probably been reached already by one of your other marketing techniques, and you shouldn't be wasting any time on them. Not to mention that Google and the other search engines do a pretty good job of making sure that your website is going to rank high on your business name by people who search within 25 miles of your location.

Never forget: you're using the Internet to get new customers who are trying to solve a problem that you and your business can solve; in short, you need to present an attractive solution to people with problems. People need help with "hair color", "make overs", or "stylist"; these are the keywords people are putting into the search box! Nobody's looking for "Shear Delight", they're looking for "haircuts" or "hair extensions", things that a beauty salon can provide a solution for. You want to rank for these keywords, and not for your business name!

2) The other big mistake we see made all the time is businesses ranking in terms that only make sense to someone who works in

that particular industry. One of the ones we've seen is the keyword phrase "Foodservice Distributor". Not many people may know to type in that food service term, as they may be more familiar with Restaurant Supply, and though they might learn about this term and start searching for that term in the future they're not doing so in great numbers right now (Google provides data about what people are searching on and while sometimes confusing to interpret -- it is free).

The most important thing to remember in keyword selection is this: you must look at keywords from the user's perspective. You can't expect them to search for the terms you believe they're going to be able to define. For example, don't ever go to your industry association definitions for keywords—unless, of course, it's to see which keywords not to use! It's a trap that many people fall into all the time, and you've got to watch out for it. Even we're not immune to it—we deal heavily in search and social media Internet marketing, and when we're not careful sometimes we find ourselves using terms people wouldn't use and don't care about: SEO, social media measurement. These are things our clients would never type in! They would type in something like "I want to get more customers" instead, and so those are the keywords we really care about.

These are the two big pitfalls that we see with most businesses that we work with, and they both stem from one thing: A lack of knowledge. Specifically, the knowledge of what people are searching for. There are a number of tools that exist out there in addition to the free Google tools, which Google has now hidden inside another tool, and they are changing all the time.

These various online tools are helpful, and clients who know how to use them will really benefit from the services they provide; the best (and fastest) way, however, to find the right keywords is just to ask your family and friends. Think back to the first chapter, when we said that it's ordinary people that are using Google; that's as true for keyword usage as it is for research methods. Ask your friends, colleagues, and neighbors for help. Ask people who know you to explain to a friend what you do and ask to listen in. They will use plain English terms to describe your business, and those are the terms that ordinary people are going to pop into that search box.

Keyword Tools:

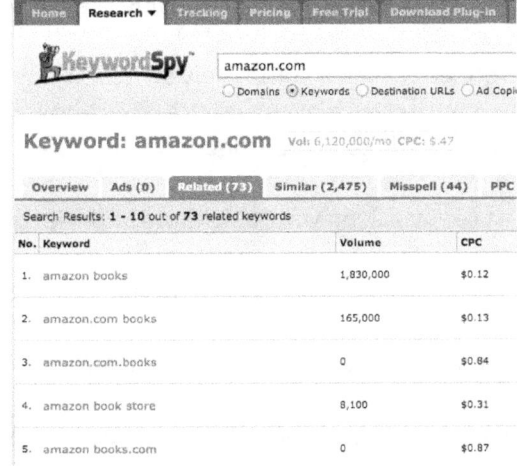

The reason this works is because it gets into the mind of a client. If you gave a 60-second description of what you do for a client, and then they turn around and tell that to a friend, it's not going to sound the same—in fact, odds are it'll be very different indeed! What you're looking for in keyword selection is not how you describe your business it's how clients and prospects describe it. If you're not ranking on the keywords that people are searching for, nobody's going to find you.

This might be a little overwhelming, but don't worry, we're not saying that you have to nail this on the first try and you can't change keywords over time. It's not the end of the world if you choose the wrong keyword at first, because keywords can be modified, refined, or even completely switched out altogether. Don't overthink your keyword selection to the point that you freeze; start off by asking your neighbors and friends, as we described above. This is a very good method to finding keywords initially, and as you get more advanced you can start using some of the tools we talked about above to refine your keyword selection. Those tools will definitely benefit, but they're not crucial right out of the gate. Start simply, as described above, and slowly grow in complexity as you master each step of the process.

Another method we use internally to refine keyword selection even further is to use Google's "Related Searches" tool. This will give you an idea of what others are searching for when they search for your keywords, potentially giving you an insight into related terms that you may not have thought of.

Another important tool in your keyword research arsenal is the Google Keyword Tool (GKT for short). The GKT is important because although the Related Searches tool gives you suggestions, the GKT gives you returns for how many people per month are actually searching for that keyword. This is across the entire USA, so you're going to have to make an educated (and usually valid) assumption that those will work in your locality very similarly to the way they work nationally. To stick to our earlier example, let's type in two terms: "Restaurant Supply" and "Foodservice Distributor".

Google AdWords

Home | **Campaigns**

Keyword Planner
Add ideas to your plan

Search terms	Avg. monthly searches
restaurant supply	33,100
foodservice distributor	40

You'll notice in the screenshot above that "Restaurant Supply" gets many more searches than "Foodservice Distributor. In fact, "Foodservice Distributor" is small enough that you may not even want to initially target it. You can assume that in your locality these numbers will probably translate fairly well. It's not a given, and there's not a great tool right now for pinpointing exact numbers of local searches, but you need to assume that the national numbers will, more or less, apply reasonably well to your local searches.

If you really want a good idea of how many local searches those national numbers signify, you can do a rough calculation: take the last census date for the total US population and take the census of your location. Divide your location by the total population and it'll give you a rough estimate of the percentage of total population- multiply that times the keywords to get your number.

For example: Let's say you live in a city with one million people. The US has 300 million, by last count, which means your city has 1/300th of the amount of searches. "Restaurant Supply" returns 30k hits per month, so we can assume that your locale's getting about 100 searches per month on that keyword. It's not exact, but it's a very good guesstimate and is often more spot-on than you'd expect!

NOTE:

Do not think that bigger is always better! Sometimes, it's better to go after an easily-dominated keyword.

The other pitfall that companies make is they typically want a neat, catchy name or their business name in the URL. If you want to rank really well, you're going to have to make your URL keyword rich.

Here's an example: Let's say you're a Financial Advisor in Phoenix, AZ, and you've decided on the keyword phrase "Financial Advisor in Phoenix AZ". A great URL for your website, then, would be "http://www. FinancialAdvisorPhoenixAZ.com". That's going to help tremendously in your efforts to rank high on Google. We realize that that's not a pretty name, and if you want to have your business name website URL for business cards and marketing materials you still can: It's both cheap and trivial to have multiple domain names, and you can easily have your webmaster redirect "http://www.jonesassociates.com" to "http://www. FinancialAdvisorPhoenixAZ.com" and still reap the benefits of the keyword-rich URL while having a professional URL on your business cards.

A keyword-rich URL is one of the first things you can do to influence your Google search rankings. We'll talk about other methods to rocket you to the top, of course, but if you start this process without a keyword-rich URL, it's going to be a very steep uphill battle. Do yourself a favor and start with a keyword-rich URL- it's very helpful and makes everything down the line much, much easier!

Niching

With this knowledge comes another facet of Internet marketing you need to know about: niching. As you may have guessed from that specific URL, you can't be highly ranked in everything. Unless you're a general practice physician in a small town, there's going to be a ton of other general practice physicians vying for that top spot in many different keywords and you're going to want to select some specialty or niche to focus on.

This isn't to say that you can't do other things or cross-sell once you get your client, but you definitely have to step back and do some business strategy when it comes to niching. Where is most of your revenue coming from? Where do you want it to come from? What's your most profitable set of business? Some things require a significant amount of time, while there are other things that an assistant can do most of the actual work: the second is often more profitable.

What it comes down to is this: To dominate online, you have to know where you want to go and <u>focus on one thing</u>. Find something that you'd be happy with if 95% of your business came from that one thing. It's there that you're going to want to start in regards to your keywords. Dominating the search rankings under pizza, ravioli, Italian food, mussels, and so forth all at once is going to be really hard, if not outright impossible. Start with the most important one, the one where you want to go: it might not be where you started, but it has to be where you want to go—the niche that you want to dominate in the future. Dominating that one keyword phrase means owning that particular source of business in your local area.

In keeping with our earlier Foodservice Distributor example: let's say you want to dominate the keyword "Restaurant Equipment". You'd make a keyword-rich URL out of that keyword-rich phrase, and then proceed to dominate the search rankings with your carefully crafted process, honed razor-sharp to focus on that particular niche.

Once you've narrowed down between 3-5 keyword phrases with a few words in them each, you'll want to make sure those keyword phrases are in your title tag in your website and that title tag starts ALWAYS with those keywords. You want the title tag to start with the keywords, move into the location, and end with the business name. Don't lead with your business name- the business name will come along for the ride. It's all over your website, and people (and Google) aren't going to miss it. Start instead with the important keywords, and make sure those are peppered all throughout your site.

TIP:

There is a time for ranking your business name and your name, for posting positive reviews and comments about you. It's called your Reputation. As a professional, people may search on your name or business name to find out more about you before contacting you to make an appointment. That's a whole subject on it's own, and very important, however, for the purposes of this chapter, we'll stick to your products and services here.

NOTE:

Don't overdo it! Google is looking for real people with real content, and not automatons who simply spew out keywords nonstop. Don't oversaturate the keywords.

Make sure your keywords hover around 4% density in the page text, which is the optimal percentage for keywords to words. (OK, we said we wouldn't try to confuse you about terms like keyword density and we just brought it up... we apologize, though you now know the specific data if you choose to use it.

However, stick with talking about your subject in a natural way and this will just work itself out.)

Another very, very important thing to think about in this strategy is whether or not you're in an area where someone else is already dominating that larger keyword phrase. If someone's dominating the keyword phrase you want, you have to focus on smaller subsets of that keyword phrase: if you can dominate 2 or 3 smaller keyword phrases, you may end up actually getting more business than the company that just went after that larger, broader term.

Those are, in effect, the two separate strategies you have to look at from an inside perspective. Everything in this book is important to understand for your business, because it makes you more knowledgeable. It enables you to do it yourself, or be savvy when you hire a business to do it for you. If you hire an outside business, you'll be able to make sure it's not just a webmaster or a designer who puts up a quick website but somebody who will ask these tough questions and really help you to think through the right online strategy for you. Just like the duplicate content we mentioned in Chapter One, there are lots of people just trying to sell something quick and dirty instead of doing things the right way—don't get fooled, make sure you're talking to someone who knows Internet marketing, and has been doing it for awhile. Remember, a website designer is more of a graphic designer, and over 90% of them do not know how to optimize that website they just designed. Don't go into any negotiations without knowing what your marketing agency should provide you.

Once you've got your keywords, your domain name, and your website ready, it's time to step up your game. Now, we're going to get into blogging to get ranked as well as more advanced local search techniques!

SUMMARY:

- Keywords are important; don't bother with trying to rank for your business name. Rank with keywords that get traffic and are terms that ordinary users are searching for!

- Incorporate your keywords into your website, and have a webmaster forward or redirect a professional-looking URL to the keyword rich one!

- Specialize, specialize, specialize, don't go for the broad market. Find your niche or specialty and aim towards that!

- Leverage your marketing tools, especially the people around you: they are, for the most part, representative of your clients and can offer insight into how your clients would search for you.

- Be natural! Google and Bing don't like keyword stuffing; don't ever go over 4% keyword density. Just write naturally, and almost always you'll have a good amount of keyword density with a natural reading flow.

4

BLOGGING AND ADVANCED LOCAL SEARCH TECHNIQUES

If you've been following this book thus far, you have a pretty reasonable setup going. In fact, you're probably better off than anybody who just slapped up a website to have an Internet presence, and you're definitely better off than anyone who has refused the transition to web-based marketing. You may even have pulled a lead or two just from having the website, and you're considering putting your Google Places / Google + Local page up right away and watch your site skyrocket to the top of those local search returns!

We like your style, but hold on to your seat—your site's still small potatoes! In this chapter, we're going to figure out how to make your local business big-time on the web using some more advanced local search techniques!

Blogging

Google has said emphatically that they're going to give stronger credit to resources that are both relevant to the user and current. This makes sense, given the overall makeup of the Internet: new content ages quickly, and very often newer information is far more useful to a person searching than old information. This problem is usually dealt with by adding new content to static web pages, but this method is time-consuming and more trouble than it's worth.

Our solution? Blogging.

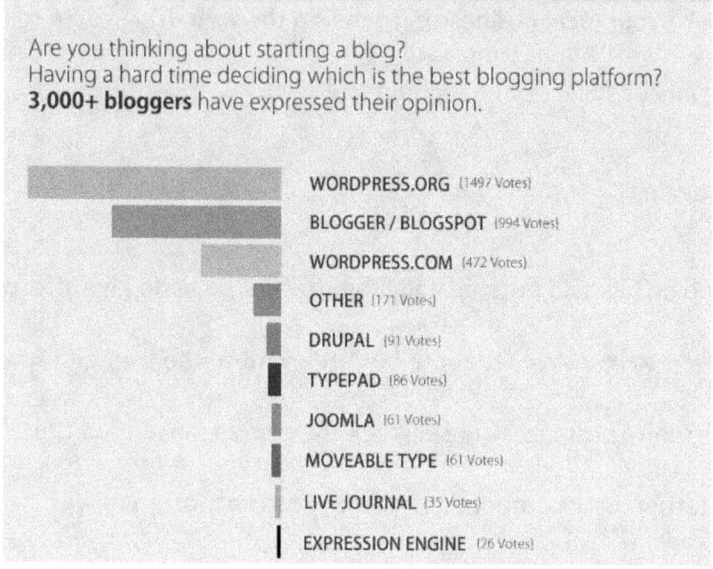

It is true that blogging has become the online activity on the Internet—it seems that everyone and their pet has one, and sometimes several. The fact of the matter is, however, blogging has become a powerful force on the Internet; it also has one distinct advantage for us in that it's by far the easiest, most convenient, and most effective way to add new, updated content to your website. You don't have to go in and change copy all the time, you don't have to deal with static pages,

HTML, and minor edits, you just have to update your blog every now and then. This again is another reason you should hire an Internet marketer for your website vs. a fancy web designer - believe me, many of them don't understand blogging, or giving you control of your own site.

It's especially helpful when you consider Google's other preference in high-ranking Google search results: steady, relevant content. There's no "magic bullet" or fast-track way to get to the top of the Google search rankings; in this case, slow and steady wins the race. Blogging is absolutely, positively 100% all about this; it's essentially a vehicle to allow you to easily make regular, useful updates to keep your site both relevant and full of a steady stream of content.

To that end, there is a minimum amount of blog posts you should be putting out each week. Because of Google's preference for updated, steady content, you should be blogging at the very least once per week, and each blog post should be between about 250-800 words; they can be longer but they don't need to be, and they definitely shouldn't be any shorter than 250 words or Google may mark them down as non-useful.

This may seem daunting to many, and understandably so; the thought of composing another written piece every week isn't appealing to many folks out there. If you truly think about it, however, once a week isn't too bad; that's only four times a month, and if you make a schedule and stick to it you'll find that blogging really isn't the chore you thought it would be.

If you're finding that you have time for more, it's beneficial to increase your blog posts to twice a week; that's the optimal number in this sort of situation, and it'll most likely net you the most positive credit when Google compiles its local search returns. Twice a week, however, is plenty; don't go over that! Some people come into this with a very linear mindset. They think that since 2 is better than 1, 5 must be better than 2. It's not, and you'll experience a very diminished rate of return in this regard; 2 blog posts a week is much better than 1, but 5 blog posts a week is barely better than 2. Bottom line is this: If you're spending more than 2 times a week blogging, there are other, better things you could be doing with that time! This goes for your assistant's time as well!

Blog Subjects

Having a blog is all well and good, but a blog without useful, relevant content is hardly a blog at all! To that end, you're going to need to fill your blog with useful, quality content that maximizes the amount of relevance Google perceives in your site. Here are the three main content points you should be hitting in your blog posts:

1) Talk About What You Do

This one may seem pretty obvious, but it's worth mentioning: talk about what you do, not who you are. Don't talk about yourself, how long your business's been around, how great your service is; this isn't going to help you any. You need to fill your blog posts with quality content that relates to the services you do, quality content is valuable and useful to the user. For example, let's say you're an Auto Repair Facility and a new product made the news recently that people are curious to find out more about. A perfect blog post would be a post covering this new product or relevant information pertaining to them; you could title it "The NEW Gas Additive and What You Need to Know" and phrase it as an easygoing, inside look at how the new service can benefit them and what that could mean for anyone looking to have that service performed.

2) Plugged in: Talk About Local Events

Number 1 on this list may seem obvious to most, but this trick isn't: of all of them, this is the super secret sauce of Internet marketing! The trick is this: talk about local events! Blogging about things going on and tying them back into what you do is a great, great way to make Google take notice and gain credit with them in the local search return results. A good example of this would be if you lived in a city and there's a big event; talk about the big event and how it related to your community. Let's say you live in a college town and every Saturday during football season the town quadruples in size. It's an event that polarizes many a college town - local residents are, in general, proud / frustrated about the big event, think it's good / bad for business? Think the traffic isn't worth the amount of money the game brings into the town? Do you have suggestions for parking or 'must hit' restaurants or activities for the in-bound football fans? You can write a blog post about this, and it'll help you with Google because Google will see that you're a part of the community and (more importantly) the blog posts gives Google lots of keyword clues about your location, really helping you to rise to the top in your location!

Additionally, don't feel pressured to make the blog post about legal issues in the community. In fact, shy away from it - these local community posts are as valuable in their own way as the legal posts you make, and someone who searches you will have plenty of time browsing your site and blog to see your other posts and find out about what you do and how you do it. This helps your business come out on top in the location it's in, because of the connection and keyword clues mentioned above; if somebody searches for "Shutters in Phoenix AZ" you'll show up because both your blog posts and your location-based (Phoenix, AZ), community-based blog posts as well. Many, many people don't do this, and that's understandable; on the surface, it doesn't make sense to talk about things that aren't related to what you do.

TIP:

You can always refer to yourself with your keywords! Don't overdo it, but it's perfectly fine to use things like "As an Estate Planner in Phoenix, Arizona, I'm always surprised when..." That's the best of both worlds!

Do I Really Need an Estate Plan?

MAY 7, 2011 BY ADMIN • LEAVE A COMMENT

An estate plan is often thought of as something that only elderly people or people with a lot of money need. But a basic estate plan is important no matter what your net worth is, and especially important if you are:

- A parent of a minor child
- A homeowner
- A small business owner
- In a committed relationship but not married
- In receipt of an inheritance of property or other assets

Even a basic estate plan will ensure your wishes are adhered to after you die.

Note use of keywords: Estate Plan and Estate Planning, but article sounds very natural

What is in an Estate Plan?

An estate plan will generally include a will, a power of attorney, a living will or health care directive, and in some cases, a trust. It's important to work with an estate planning attorney licensed in your state, as there are state, as well as federal, laws that govern estates.

Everyone needs a will, which can be a relatively simple document that describes where you want your assets distributed when you die, and who you would want to take care of your children. If you die without a will, the process of closing and distributing the estate will be costly and time consuming for your heirs, and you will have no control over how your assets are distributed.

Trusts are often created at the same time as a will, and that is because they are an excellent tool to allow you to put conditions on how and when your assets will be distributed. A trust can greatly speed the process of asset distribution, and reduce the cost. Trusts are not just for the rich n they are for anyone who has assets they want to distribute.

A Little Preparation Goes a Long Way

A good place to start is by thinking about all of your assets, including real estate, investments, retirement savings and life insurance policies, and then thinking about who you would want to inherit these assets. You should also consider who you would want to handle your finances and medical treatment decisions if you should become incapacitated. And of course, you will want to carefully consider who you would want to be the guardian to any minor children in the event of your death.

If there are charities that you support, including them in your estate planning is an excellent way to leave a gift that can have a lasting impact. Your estate planning advisor can help you structure this type of gift most effectively.

Finally, to save confusion and heartache later on, be clear and communicate with your heirs about your plans. A little communication goes a long way in avoiding arguments and rifts.

To find an estate planning attorney, most state bar web sites have listings of attorneys licensed to practice in that state. Referrals from friends and relatives are often the best way to ensure that you find an advisor who will help make your wishes come true, even after you're gone.

Another great tip is to be proactive. Go to a local newspaper site, see what they're covering, and link back to the newspaper site and talk about it. It's easy research!

This also has the added advantage of making you seem more likeable and down-to-earth, which is always a huge bonus in client interaction. When someone finds your blog and reads through it, it'll be enjoyable- she'll be getting not just practical advice but also feel some connection to you as well. When she reads your blog, she won't see just another faceless professional - she'll read your blog posts about the community and think "Gee, this person has personality. They seem to really know what they are talking about, AND they are also a part of my community and seem really invested in it."

That person is more likely to pick up the phone and give you a call, and you just got a warm lead by being a personable blogger who talks about the community!

3) Be Natural

This ties into the last point—be natural! You don't always have to sound like the smartest person in the world on your blog.

This isn't to say you should be sloppy or stupid, but you shouldn't sound like a ruler preaching from atop the mountain either. Your clients (and Google) like to see content and blog posts that appear and are from everyday type people. Conversation, stories, and anecdotes are all things they like to index; conversing on your blog makes you more reachable and more index-able.

This isn't just a Google-specific tactic, either; your customers will love you for it as well, as we mentioned above. It's always been a general marketing strategy to be likeable; it's the age-old marketing concept that people are more likely to work with those similar to themselves. They see your blog posts and say, "Hey! This person knows what they're talking about and likes what I like." They see a real person, with a real family, and it makes them feel more comfortable working with you. A blog is the best place to do this, so plan out your blog structure accordingly. You don't have to do 52 weeks of straight specialty talk; you can do every now and then an informal, "Hey, somebody asked me about this the other day and I thought I'd talk about it" post.

A good rule of thumb, if you're doing the minimum four times a month, is to split it up half and half: twice a month goes to business posts, and twice a month goes to local, personal stories. People like to know people, it's a fact of interaction; it will greatly help your sales when they feel that they know you more personally. This tactic may feel a little too touchy-feely for some, but don't knock it: it works very well, and blogging is a great way to do it! It drives clients and will improve your ranking, which is of course a major goal of this book.

What you should really take from this chapter is to not underestimate the power of the local connection. We've had clients that have followed this process to the letter, and their specialty posts only gained a few hits and comments. It was their local stories and blog posts, however, which became a focal point. Conversations about how bad the traffic was when a big event happened got tons of links, comments, and opinions from across the board.

In the end, this is what you want: it's the reason for this section and the reason you're branching out into the community. Not only does this sort of activity tied into your locality keywords mean big index boosts from Google, it also means very effective general marketing: it makes you a real person that people feel comfortable calling, one of the best advantages you can have in our modern, very skeptical era!

SUMMARY:

- Blogging is key to the success of your marketing campaign: make sure to blog at least once a week with a post that is between 250 and 800 words. If you have time, it is better to blog twice a week. This is the optimal number, and blogging more than twice a week won't help you more.

- You don't have to make every blog about your business; you should alternate them between your business and events in the community.

- Be natural; this will help you be more accessible to your customers, and thus garner more page views and attention from people looking to comment on the blog as well as make you more viewable and index-able by search engines.

5

USING FACEBOOK, TWITTER, LINKDIN AND OTHER PLATFORMS

We know some of you are snickering. We know some of you are sitting in your home or offices, having read the title of this particular chapter, and are thinking "Twitter! That can't possibly help me."

Don't laugh just yet, however: We know how silly Twitter sounds. We know the derision it's received from all sides, including our friends and the media; the fact of the matter is, however, that Twitter is relevant. As much as it pains us to say, Twitter may be one of the more important factors that figures into your Internet marketing strategy.

Wow! So you better get tweeting!

Why Social Media?

Simply put: Social media is starting to become a very powerful force in how Google is determining what is relevant online. The Internet is full of bots, scammers, and article spinners, and many links out there are links to irrelevant or otherwise 'spammy' articles. Social media, however, does the vetting by itself: Users of social media sites aren't going to share 'spammy' links with each other, they're going to share real content. As a result, Google has realized that indexing and calculating relevancy from social media is very beneficial, since social media (in general) has real people posting real content, content that was valuable enough to warrant a "hey, check this out" from one person to another.

Some of us have been trying to avoid social media for one reason or the other: privacy, general lack of interest or time, or whatever other reason you may have avoided it thus far. The statistics on social media and Internet marketing, however, can't be denied: for example, By 2010 Gen Y will outnumber Baby Boomers…. 96% of them have joined a social network. These are the people that look for you, and by ignoring the social media segment you're basically ignoring their primary mode of access. This will put a practice out of business eventually!

- The average time on Google is three minutes. The average time on Facebook is thirteen minutes.

- Facebook, as of this writing, has over 1.19 billion users. To put that into perspective, that means Facebook has more users than the US population; this is very important in terms of saturation.

What these statistics should show you is that social media is a very, very powerful force in today's cultural mindset, and it's only getting stronger. Social media is here to stay, and more and more people every day are joining it and receiving advice from their friends and family about great stories or services that they received. Good old word of mouth is alive and well!

Google has been taking notice of that and responding accordingly, and so should you. In this chapter, we're going to take a look at social networks and your strategy for them: we're going to figure how just to approach these social media platforms and use them to help Google notice you!

The Social Networks

In the social media game, there are currently three huge players that we're going to focus on: Facebook, Twitter, and LinkedIn. This isn't to say you should ignore the other social media networks out there; they're still important, and in fact location-based social media like Foursquare and Facebook Places are very useful too. You may want to have a presence in those, and other minor social networks as well, like Google+, etc.

For the core of our marketing strategy, however, we're going to focus on the big three. This focus will give you the most coverage and best ROI in terms of time spent on marketing, and so it's how we'll proceed!

Facebook

Facebook's the biggest social media in the room, the 800-pound gorilla; everybody knows and uses it, so you're going to need to capitalize on that. The first thing you should have is a fan page, and so we'll take a look at how to create one and how to link it into your overall Internet marketing strategy.

TIP:

Many of you will be scared of Facebook's privacy implications. It's very important to note that your business fan page is NOT your personal page. It's not the same thing as your personal page, and nothing you post on your personal page will appear on your business page or vice versa. They are completely separate entities! For those you of you resisting joining Facebook and are afraid your fan page will expose your personal page, fear not: none of your personal information will go on your fan page, and your privacy is safe.

Your Facebook Fan Page

A fan page, quite simply, represents your business. Facebook fan pages can have dynamic pages that offer info about your business- you're going to want someone to build a custom 'iframe' on the landing page for your fan page (An iframe is a special box on a web page with content from another source). Your web developer or webmaster should be able to do this pretty easily. When new visitors come to the fan page they will see the information in the iframe, which will be an opt-in box and benefit information; this will be very similar to the call to action you have on your main website - "3 Things to Know Before You Call an "Exterminator", that sort of thing.

The great part of this fan page is that you're adding new clients onto an email marketing list through a social media channel. It's a very organic way of getting warm leads and targeted marketing. These people are already in the social media world, surfing around, and in their social network traversal they stumble on your fan page and think "Wow! I might need a Plumber for my leaky faucet". In fact, the #1 growing demographic of Facebook is 25-34 and 35-54 year old females.

This is a massive, growing target market for many, many people who need a product or service for all kinds of reasons. It's definitely the right mix of people with the money and the motive to hire a professional, and your fan page on Facebook will be a great place for them to get in touch with you regarding their problems.

While you're creating your Facebook fan page, don't forget about your Facebook Places page as well. The location-based aspect of this is really attractive, especially because of the proliferation of mobile phones. More and more people are buying smartphones and more and more things are going mobile. With a Places page, people can check in and see what's around them, and you can offer specials through this mode of delivery. At least get on this platform, but you can take it further - be creative! Combine things like your Fan page and

Places page, and figure out ways to synergize the two to make an effective marketing vehicle!

This is perhaps the most important thing to know about social media in general; all of these things can be linked together in different ways. There are so many options for managing Fan pages and Places pages that it's vital you have a professional who knows how to set up social media correctly. Barring that, you need to get online and do some extensive research into establishing the proper social media channels; it's not something you can just toss together quickly.

Once you've got your Fan page and Places set up, it's time to move on.

Twitter

Twitter—one of the newest social networks out there, and perhaps one that inspires the most reluctance to join. It's been downplayed by the media and our peers, but the fact remains that Twitter is important: it's the most open social network out there.

In fact, this is the whole reason Twitter is so important. Every single tweet (a "tweet" is what each individual Twitter post is called) is indexed by Google. Other social networks, like Facebook and LinkedIn, need a username and password to see most of their content; with Twitter, there's no requirement to log in to see individual tweets. What this means is that Google can index all the tweets out there, and this means that Twitter affects Google page rankings enormously; Google is using people's tweets to help gauge the importance of pages all around the Internet. Pages with lots of links from Twitter, for example, are going to increase its importance: you don't want to be 'spammy', but you do want to take advantage of this fact.

That's the basis of most of your Twitter interaction, when it's all said and done: taking advantage of Twitter's ability to generate constant content without coming across as being 'spammy'. You can't just blast out links to your blog articles all day; a stream of useless / irrelevant content from you (or rehashed content) isn't going to help you to increase your page rank.

You're going to want to create a bunch of tweets about local things like events as well as topical content like minor changes, changes that would be important or useful for people to know. Your tweets are going to be composed of similar content to your blogs, except shortened down to the 140 character limit per tweet, and sent out once or twice a day.

This may seem as daunting as the blogging, especially considering the daily frequency of the tweets. Truth be told, however, 140 characters is not that much at all, and you don't have to sit by the computer and send them out one by one; there are tons of programs that let you schedule tweets, including HootSuite (http://hootsuite.com), SocialOomph (http://www.socialoomph.com), and more. You can sit down for an hour and write enough tweets for a week or two, schedule them, and forget about them until the next week when you sit down to write some more!

Don't be tempted just to tweet an exact duplicate of your blog posts or articles! Your tweets should be on the same content as your blog posts, but they shouldn't be copied and pasted straight from the blog. What you can do, however, is to link back to your blog from your tweets: in fact, this is not only permissible but encouraged! There are many, many plugins for countless blogging platforms that enable you to automatically send out a tweet with a link to your blog post every time you post a new blog post. Take advantage of that to generate links to your blog posts—that's not 'spammy' since it's only once or twice a week, and it's a great tool for slowly and steadily creating links back to your blog. There are also plugins for Facebook as well—make sure when you post a blog, it's getting automatically posted to your Twitter and Facebook page!

LinkedIn

In the social media circles, LinkedIn is often completely overshadowed by its bigger social media cousins Facebook and Twitter. It is instead regarded as just a professional or resume-sharing site and nothing more; this is a big misstep for many, as LinkedIn is an enormous cash cow if used properly. For starters,

LinkedIn itself is no slouch in terms of financial recognition; now publicly traded (LNKD), Linked In has a market cap of $8-$10 billion (or $70-$100 per user)—making it a very formidable, fast-growing contender in the social media sphere.

Additionally, LinkedIn has an added attraction to us that isn't related to its market share. Because of LinkedIn's status as a site for professionals and resume-swapping, the average LinkedIn user is far more likely to be a potential client because of the means / motive aspect we described earlier with Facebook.

1. Over one fifth of users are Middle Management level or above
2. Almost 60% have a College or Post Grad degree
3. Average Household Income is $88,573.
4. All of these numbers are higher than published statistics on Wall Street Journal, Forbes, or BusinessWeek.

Put simply, LinkedIn users are wealthier and require more services, and non-useful demographics, like teenagers, aren't crowding the LinkedIn user space to post pictures of their friends and pets. LinkedIn is composed of your potential clients interacting with each other, looking for professionals and just waiting to be introduced to your business.

Press Releases

This isn't really social media, but we're going to incorporate it into this section because it deals with controlling a message that goes out and can get shared and receive comments; in a sense, the medium of the Internet itself is social. PR is also one of the few places where Google expects duplicate content; the more duplicated/shared the press release is, the more important the content must be.

15 Great Press Release Ideas:

1. Someone in your company is speaking at an industry conference, local chamber, rotary club, etc.

2. You hire someone new into your company

3. Someone is promoted

4. You join an association (local or national)

5. You start offering a new service or product

6. New office space or additional office added

7. Successful client -- create a Case Study and send out press release

8. Awards received or recognition from local or national industry or association

9. Employee or officers named to charity benefit or non-profit board

10. Large sponsor of a charity benefit

11. New Business contract awarded

12. Announcing a big promotion, sweepstakes or contest

13. Your product and services tie into a big current event news item (new government law, health discovery, tax time, new hot-topic, movie release, etc.)

14. Launch of a new website (hint, hint)

15. The release of your special report (hint hint)

There are both paid and free press sites out there; the paid press sites are worth the money sometimes because they go out to Associated Press and other big name news wires, like Yahoo and Google News. The more that your story gets out there, the more possibility it is that it could get picked up; a local paper could see that press release and pick up the story, for example, and that's a great thing to take advantage of. The problem of duplicate content goes out the window because duplicate content is expected in press releases, and often the big names, like Associated Press and Reuters, even publish duplicate content!

GOOGLE+:

What makes Google+ different from Facebook, LinkedIn, YouTube and Twitter?

This is not Google's first attempt at social. There are many social networks, but let's focus on the big four Facebook, Linkedin, YouTube and Twitter. Understanding how these sites operate helps explain Google+.

YouTube – I make a video. You search for it and can watch, share, or comment on my video. As a search based network this is the most open network of them all, however few people use the subscribe function as a social element.

LinkedIn – It used to be: Here is my resume, please hire me – Now it is: I need a job, I collaborate with my colleagues & vendors to learn and grow in groups, and I get / answer questions. The most closed network of the four, you must know my email, already have worked with me, or be in a group with me to connect.

Twitter – I can push information out to many people and this information can be spread quickly. Google indexes this network, which is a bonus. As many people as are on Twitter can follow my updates. You can follow me and I do not need to follow you. Information is sent out in short bursts and interactions. These take place both on Twitter (in a short conversation style) and off Twitter (follow this link to see this video, read my blog, etc)

Facebook - The current king of social media. Facebook is about "friendships". You and I must mutually like each other to share information. I can post information with hopes that this information is seen on your News Feed. There is no guarantee my information will be seen by my friends. Facebook controls information and uses an algorithm called Edge to determine what information they believe I want to see. There is a great business component with Pages (formally fan pages).

Google+ What makes you so different?

From a big picture standpoint Google+ is about connecting all of your computer uses both online and offline in one place. We are talking cloud on a major scale. We are talking about your documents, spreadsheets, applications, videos, everything being available in one location and everything being one click from something you can share.

This brings us to the MAJOR DIFFERENCE of Google+

So this is great, I can share all my information from my blog to my expense report, but I don't want to share everything with the world. My mom does not need to know about everything about work and my clients don't want to know about my personal life.

Google+ has created a revolutionary function called CIRCLES. Circles control both the stream of information out and in. People you connect with are organized into different circles.

How do Circles work and why are they important?

1) You can create any circle you want. Examples of my circles include: Following, Friends, Employees, Clients, Vendors, Other Smart Marketing People, Fellow Medical and Professional Marketers, and Family.

2) The people you connect with can be in multiple circles. Some people that are Smart Marketing People are also my Friends.

3) I can choose to send information to one, or more, circles. This information will appear on their wall or can be sent as a message. The great thing is if I share something with my client circle, only them and no one else sees that post on their feed.

Maybe we just got back from a family vacation and I want to share the photos with my family and friends but do not want to bother my vendors, clients, and the general public with the images.

4) I can choose to see information from one or more circles in my feed. Instead of being told what content an algorithm thinks I would like to see, I can choose my content feed based on my circles. This allows me to quickly and easily navigate from one set of feeds to the next. Since you can have people in multiple circles, I know that I am seeing what I want from whom I want.

Here are a few other features to Google+

- Multiple Video Chat. Google+ will allow you to connect with up to ten people on live video chat at the same time. The feature is smooth and audio is good. A real great way to connect with people for virtual meetings. The best part of this feature is the person talking gets the main screen. These are called Google Hangouts.

- Larger image and video display on the wall. When you post a video or images they are about three times larger on the wall when compared to Facebook.
- Easy navigation to all of Google's functions. While on Google+ you can search the web, see your gmail messages, and access your Google Documents.
- Simple share option. This is very similar to Facebook. Google uses both a +1 button (similar to Facebook's like) and a "share this post" option.
- One click and you can add someone. If you see a name in a post, find someone in your friends feed, or stumble upon someone of interest you can add them without navigating to their page. This is very convenient. When you hover over their name you a box appears giving you the option to add them to a circle.

Setting up Google+ is simple. Similar to other social media outlets, there is an area for information about you, pictures, website URLs, and basic data. As always, only share what you are comfortable sharing. Make sure your "about me" section has benefits to working with you and keywords for your industry. Like LinkedIn there is a title area that you should also include keywords about your area of practice.

The difficult part about social media is that it is rapidly changing.

Press Releases are so important to the overall online strategy that we've started writing, publishing, and syndicating releases on behalf of our clients. Once again, we found that the average business owner had better things to do than to write press releases all day. Maybe you have the time - our clients certainly don't. Either way, press releases have to be a part of the overall success strategy online.

With that, our journey into social media has ended; next up on our list is directory listings!

SUMMARY:

- Social media is one of the most important forces in marketing today: it can't afford to be ignored, and you need to set up strategies for dealing with it.

- The three biggest social media players right now are Facebook, Twitter, and LinkedIn: you need to have pages for them and have a system set up on your blog that pushes blog updates to the respective social networks.

- Google+, though new, is rapidly growing: make sure to incorporate it into your marketing strategy!

- Press releases are an extremely important part of your online marketing strategy, so much so that you should have your marketing agency do it for you and cut down on the immense amount of time you're spending on it.

- Social media is rapidly changing, and no single strategy will stay effective forever; make sure to keep yourself updated to stay ahead of the curve!

6

HOW TO USE ONLINE DIRECTORIES TO GET MORE CLIENTS

If you've been an Internet user since the pre-search days, you'll recognize directory listings. Directory listings are, in short, the online version of the Yellow Pages: Super Pages, YellowPages.com, Yahoo Local, Bing Places, Google Places / Google + Local, etc. These directories are commonly called "citations" by those in the Internet marketing and search marketing industry. There are hundreds of them across the Internet; there are, however, 12-15 major ones where you want to be listed.

The main directories are MerchantCircle.com, SuperPages.com,

Yelp.com, and Yahoo Local. There are also industry specific directories you should be should be sure to get listed in. The majority of these services allow for a free listing. You should not need anything more than that. Resist being upsold from all of the follow-up emails and phone calls trying to upsell you to upgrade to a paid option. A paid listing or preferred listing may be right for you depending on your market, but do everything else first. Then after you have a baseline for your online success, test the gain in calls or emails you receive by opting for a paid enhancement to a directory listing. That way you can measure the real cost/benefit of the investment and make the best choice for your business.

Some directories, like InfoUSA, are even more influential and you must be sure your information is correct and optimized. The reason why is that other directories pull information from them, so over time, as other directories use the information there, your information will proliferate all over the Internet. Make sure it is the right information.

These directories/citations have risen to prominence lately because of Google's local search return policies, since Google has moved its local search returns to its main page, using Google Places / Google + Local. The algorithm that determines which Google Places / Google + Local business listings belong on the first page of Google search results takes a great deal of its weighting consideration by looking around the Internet to see if your business is listed elsewhere. If you're in 5, 10, or even 15 directory listings (with reviews in the local area) that's going to look very good in Google's ranking system.

We'll get to reviews in the next chapter, but suffice it to say that directory listings with reviews are very helpful; if your competition is getting more reviews than you, you often won't make the first page and they will! Reviews are also becoming more important because of this.

You're going to want to be in many directories. There are some services out there that will do this for you, but quite often the best way to do it is to do it manually. You really want to be in control of this—some services are pretty spotty in this regard, and they'll slip in shady techniques or insist that you stay out of the process. It's not that hard, but it is time-consuming, and we recommend doing it manually. Here's how. Just go through the top 10-15 directory listings, enter in your data, put photos, and fill out the details as much as you can. Make sure to use keywords and geo-location in your description (geo-location is just an SEO term for city / state). In keeping with our Financial Services example, if you're a Financial Advisor in Phoenix, AZ and your keywords are "Financial Investor", you could put in your description "Financial Investor in Phoenix, Arizona". Another key to remember here too is to use the exact same information in each one. If you spell your street name out in one, then do not abbreviate it in another, etc.

How to List Yourself

It's a pretty easy process to list your self in directories. You just have to go to these directories and their websites, and list yourself. Some are paid, but many are free and just try to upcharge you with different services once you've listed your company. You may be conflicted about these upcharges and paid directory listings, but they're really not necessary. Our experience is that, done correctly, you never need to pay for directory listings or any of the extra services the free ones offer you; judicious and skillful use of keywords and geo-location will be more than enough to bump you up to the top.

We've had many, many clients top-ranked in Google Places / Google + Local who never paid for directory listings, and it's most likely the case that you'll never have to pay for a directory listing or upcharge either. That is not to say that these additional paid services won't provide more traffic and clients to your business, but don't start there.

Be warned, however: you will get multiple phone calls from those directories looking to sell you upcharges and service add-ons. Changes to Google and other advertising venues online have left many of these directories rethinking their business models and scrambling by the wayside; paying for a directory listing is no longer as necessary as it used to be. You'll have many directories telling you to upcharge this and upcharge that and pay for advertising, but don't do it: and you'll see that it wasn't necessary at all to pay for any services that the directory listings tried to offer you!

NOTE:

Big warning here! This is a problem that we run into with many local businesses. What happens is that often with an executive suite, you have three or four professionals in one location. If each of them go in and create their own listing, you end up with multiple listings for each professional and one for the office suite as a whole. When Google queries the directory listings, it gets confused at the multiple entries for the one address; it thinks it's an attempt to game the system and may ignore them all.

You want to go in and be very, very careful that you only have one listing; search for your address, business name, other people in the office, anything you can think of to identify multiple listings. If you do have multiple listings and didn't know it, delete them all! Get down to zero and start from scratch; it's much better that way. If for whatever reason you can't delete them all, at least get down to one and edit that one as best you can.

It used to be a big trick to list duplicate listings to boost search rankings, and so now Google cracks down on it very hard. Remember: duplicate listings are bad! Too many dupes, and Google completely ignores them all. Be very wary of this, and search hard for duplicate listings!

Another important thing to remember when you're doing directory listings is to make sure to use keywords and geo-location only in the short or long descriptions that the directory listings give you. Do not use keywords in your business name! This is why you have a keyword-rich URL - if the URL was the business name you'd have to use that and not get the keyword benefit. Google does not like to see business names stuffed with keywords and geo-location; that will definitely hurt you in the long run.

This can be turned to your advantage, depending on how dedicated you are to this strategy; some of our sharper clients have actually changed their business name to include keywords and geo-location, like "Realtor of Scottsdale AZ". This may bring back memories from the Yellow Pages game of putting A's in business names to get to the top of the listings, like "AA Best Realtor of Scottsdale, AZ".

If your company name officially contains your keywords and location, Google is OK with that; what they're watching out for is obvious keyword stuffing like "Jones Landscape – tree trimming – grass mowing – irrigation systems - Phoenix AZ". That's bad, and those keywords should go in your description and not in your business name.

If the directory listing has suggested keywords, consider using them; it probably looks very similar to the Yellow Pages categories you are used to seeing. Some places give you a chance to type in yours, in which case do so. Don't go crazy, however, because Google only values about 3-4 keywords; anything after that they consider gaming the system and just ignore.

Here's the top directories your business should be listed on:

1. Google Places / Google + Local

2. Yahoo!

3. YellowBot

4. Yelp

5. WhitePages

6. MapQuest

7. SuperPages

8. CitySearch

9. YellowBook

10. Local.com

11. MerchantCircle

There are about 40 more directory listings that we list our clients on. Some of these directory listings are more relevant today then a year from now. Do some research and find at least 15 more directories to list your business on top of the core 11 above.

Google Places / Google + Local

Google Places / Google + Local, though technically a listing, deserves a special mention here. The Google Places / Google + Local listing should be the absolute last thing you should create; get the rest of the directory listings in first, wait a month or so until you have a few reviews, and then create your Google Places / Google + Local page. This wait time is very important- it's so important, in fact, that if we meet clients who already have a Google Places / Google + Local listing before this structure is in place we sometimes advise them to delete it and start over unless it's already in the top 7 listings. If it's not on the first page, delete it, do this process, and then add it a month later.

The reason behind this is that when you create a Google Places / Google + Local page, it goes forth and looks for all the information about you: directory listings, blogs, reviews, etc. and so forth. If you've done all the things we've talked about it should help rocket way up to the top of the list once you create it. If you want to be on the first page, waiting those four weeks to make a Google Places / Google + Local listing makes a huge, huge difference in your ranking!

Also, another powerful, yet rarely discussed advertising medium is Pay Per Click advertising... the best example of which is Google AdWords. AdWords is pound-for-pound the single quickest way to get your business listed on Page #1 of Google. You can do it in 10 minutes or less. It will cost you a few dollars a day (when you know what you are doing). Or it could cost you thousands (if you don't). The key is to have your ads show ONLY in your geographical area. Our recommendation is to find someone who is skilled at AdWords and pay them to do your ads. It will pay off for you in the end.

SUMMARY:

- There are hundreds of directory listings out there; be smart and only join the 10-15 that are the biggest and most relevant (Yelp, etc.)

- You can pay people to put you on directories, but the most cost effective way is to do it yourself. However, if you're not sure of the keywords that are being searched the most, and not skilled at copying the exact same information about your practice into the many directories, then find a good internet marketer to do this for you. Most directories are free. They'll try to get you with up-sells and add-ons, but don't bother. They don't help.

- Don't put keywords in your business name in the directories; Google doesn't like it unless those keywords are officially part of your business name.

- You'll be tempted to put up a Google Places / Google + Local along with the directories, but don't. Since Google pulls information about you when you create the Google Places / Google + Local page, it's best to wait a month or so and create one after you've gotten a few reviews.

7

HOW TO USE ONLINE REVIEWS TO DRIVE YOUR MARKETING

This part of the system really confuses some people, especially since reviews are created by clients and customers. How can reviews make or break a search engine ranking? Sure, they might be helpful for clients talking to clients, but they surely can't influence Google's monstrous ranking machine in your favor. Can they?

As it turns out, they can and they do influence the ranking system. Very much so, in fact; Google uses reviews in order to judge the validity of the place in question. Put simply, if the location's been reviewed, someone's been there, and the review comments also give an indication of the quality of the location and whether or not it deserves to be ranked higher or lower. Many of these reviews allow reviewers to give star ratings, which are even more influential: Google scrapes these numbers automatically to do a sort of website litmus test, a judgment of whether or not the establishment is overall positive or negative.

In fact, Google has recently adjusted the Google Places / Google + Local page user interface to prominently display the "Write a review" button to specifically encourage reviews within Google's own systems.

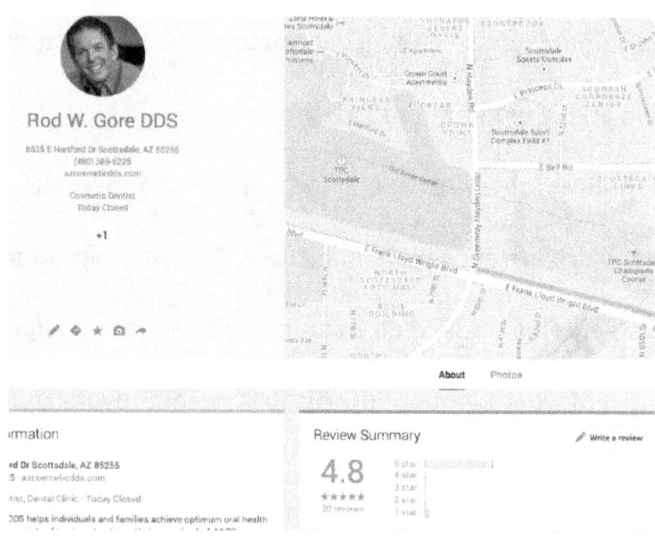

Review sites are, in general, the directory listings we talked about earlier; Google uses the information to determine whether or not you're the best solution to the problem that the user is trying to solve. This is important - the whole idea of the ranking system and your marketing strategy is to make Google see that you are, in fact, the best solution to the problem!

Another key point to this strategy is that many of your competitors are simply not getting reviews at all.

Rod W. Gore DDS
8535 E Hartford Dr, Scottsdale, AZ
(480) 585-6225 · azcosmeticdds.com
4.8 ★★★★★ 28 reviews ·

Scottsdale Center For Dental Medicine (Via De Ventura Dental Care)
8415 N Pima Rd #125, Scottsdale, AZ
(480) 948-4445 · scottsdalecdm.com
3 reviews ·
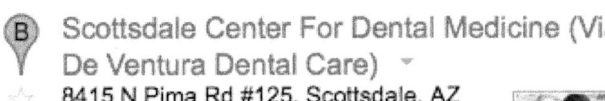

Dr. Steven H. Poulos, DDS
9070 E Desert Cove Ave, Scottsdale, AZ
(480) 614-1122 · myscottsdaledentist.com
3.4 ★★★★ 5 reviews ·

Brannon Reed DDS
8591 E Bell Rd #101, Scottsdale, AZ
(480) 367-0300 · scottsdaleazdentist.com
4.8 ★★★★★ 22 reviews ·
office staff · great team · invisalign · anxiety

Scottsdale Family Dentistry; Dental Works, PC
9070 E Desert Cove Ave, Scottsdale, AZ
(480) 391-0099 · dentalwork.com
1 review ·
new patients · oral surgery · invisalign
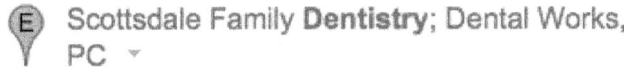

American Family Dentistry
14201 N Hayden Rd, Scottsdale, AZ
(480) 998-4867 · dentistryofarizona.com
3.7 ★★★★ 8 reviews ·
dental experience · restorative

Scottsdale Dental Care
7600 E Camelback Rd, Scottsdale, AZ
(480) 949-5727 · scottsdaledentalcare.net
4 reviews ·
dr thompson · latest technology · teeth whitening · denture · veneers
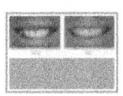

Notice that many of these businesses have no reviews, or a low number of them! As a result, you don't need to get a thousand reviews on your directory listings and Google Places / Google + Local page; you just need to have a little consistency and make sure you're getting a couple reviews a month on just 2 or 3 different directories (one of which must be Google Places / Google + Local).

To start, you're going to need to size up how many reviews you need to rank. Do some review research on your keywords; type them into Google and see how many reviews the top ranked results have. If they have five reviews, you need ten - if they have two hundred, well... you've got a lot of work to do! For the most part, in order to beat them at the rankings game, you'll need to have about double the amount of reviews they have.

Keep in mind that these are total reviews: for example, if you need twenty reviews, you can spread it over four months. That's just five reviews per month, which is certainly doable, and we'll talk about how to get those reviews in a second.

Review Sites

First things first, however, on which sites should you be focusing on getting reviews? There are tons of them out there, and some of them don't matter and some of them do. How do you figure out which ones are worth your time and which ones aren't?

Thankfully, there's a fairly efficient way to do it. First off, half the work is done: many of these review sites are also directory listings, and you've already listed yourself on the top directory listings. What you have to do, then, is to do a Google keyword search in your location and go through the pages at the bottom.

Don't go digging too far; you're rarely going to have to go digging down through the pages. If you scroll down to the bottom, you'll see numbers as far as the mouse can click. For your part, you're just interested in the top five directories that are already listed; make a list of your directory listings and cross-reference which ones appear first in the Google keyword search. For example, if you are a pool supply in Mesa AZ, then you should Google "Pool Supply Mesa AZ – your business name". Then look at the results and find the first 3-5 listings that refer to an online directory site like Yelp, CitySearch, or SuperPages. The 3-5 that appears first are the ones you're going to want to focus on.

It's also OK if you don't find 5; you may only find 2 or 3 at the beginning, and that's fine. This is normal - sometimes it can take search engines quite some time to properly index all the information out there. To give you some perspective, there are about ten thousand new websites created every day; this is a gigantic amount for search engines to index, and so often there's a lag time as the search engines crawl the pages and index them. Your mission here is to find the ones that are ranked, and of those find the top ranked ones; these are the ones where you're going to focus your review techniques!

TIP:

If there are a great number of reviews for your keyword niche, consider focusing on one or two. If you have a competitor that's saturated with reviews, Google search their keywords and see which review sites are consistently being pulled up the most; focus all your review efforts on those. As an example, if your keyword is "Pool Supply, Mesa, AZ" and the majority of reviews are being pulled from CitySearch, then CitySearch is the best place to start.

Getting Reviews

Now that we've narrowed down our target directories, let's get reviews on them. We'll start with your current clients: it'll be easier to get reviews from them, as they're right in the middle of working with you.

It's important to note here that we understand that some business professionals are, depending on the state, sometimes not allowed to ask for testimonials. You need to understand this because this is important: you are not asking for a testimonial. We are very clear on this point: you are simply asking for someone to go to a website and put in a review. It's on a public forum where they could leave the review with or without your assistance. You're going to want to have a card produced, see our sample below, that you hand to your clients as they walk out the door; this card will tell them where to go and how to write a review. This is absolutely crucial!

NOTE:

You cannot, under any circumstances, go in to these websites and create the reviews for your clients. They also can't give you the reviews offline and then you type the reviews online for them. Google will know from the IP address that these reviews are all coming from the same location and they will ignore it at best and hurt your ranking or get rid of your listing altogether at the worst. This is true even if they are real reviews that clients mailed you. A common scammer trick is to have teams of people writing multiple reviews, and as such Google is searching that spam out, and penalizing it harshly. Under no circumstances should your clients write reviews from your location; they have to go to their computer at their house, business, or coffee shop and write the review there. This is vital!

This also extends to other computers in your office. There is a common setup we see fairly often - businesses will have a "review" computer set up in the office, where clients can go and enter in a review. This falls into the same trap as the scenario above, and we always warn clients against this when we see it. Google is tracking these reviews, and even though it's not you typing, unfortunately, it's coming from the same place. Google can't distinguish these from scammers who employ that same trick, and thus having this "review station" isn't going to help you at all. They absolutely, positively have to do it on their computer in their home or business; there's no way around this and it's very important for you to remember this!

NOTE:

Be very, very, very careful about whom you hire to do your review process! There are many services out there that will solicit you and claim to be able to get you lots of reviews. Very often, these services are near-spam type businesses that just create all the reviews themselves and post them from one IP address. Not only is this not going to help you, this sort of review fabrication is against the law. You have to be very careful about who you consult and how. If you talk to a company that says they'll get you twenty reviews in a week, you should be very cautious. We've even seen reviews from businesses we've worked with that have used such services, and the result shows 20 reviews for different businesses that are all just the same sentence with the business name replaced.

Make sure you build your process with a proven agency / partner. We provide our clients with an entire review process strategy and service.

As an example of this, we have a process where we do calling / mailers for the clients depending on their individual needs. We keep close communication with the client and have an active role due to the nature, sensitivity, and importance of reviews. This is how your service should treat you. Make sure the service keeps very close to your business and gives your business the ultimate control over the review process. This is a crucial part of hiring a service—don't forget it whenever you're looking around for these agencies or services.

And.. because you purchased this book, if you are interested in having one of our partners personally review your website and online strategy, simply mention this book and receive your $200 value "Speed to Market Session" with our compliments!

Just go to www.123MarketingResults.com/coupon – this URL gives you a coupon that makes this $200 strategy session free for you, since you are reading and implementing the things in this book. Note, while it's free, we're busy, and availability may be limited. It's a great opportunity to get your online presence reviewed by one of our experts.

The best way to get these reviews, as mentioned above, is to hand out your card. Don't stop there, however... another great way is mailing or emailing clients asking for reviews (see our sample below). Make it a team effort - insert into the email where you're ranking and where your competitors are ranking, and explain that you want to get to the top and get reviews as well.

```
===================================================================
```
Subject:
What does ice cream and Law have in common?

Body:
There are always a million flavors to choose from, but when you find one you like you stick with it. We all have our favorite ice cream and we hope that our firm is your favorite.

We are writing you today to say hello and wish you the best. As part of our efforts to continue to provide the best service to our clients we need to ask you for a quick favor.

Take a moment and go to one of the websites below and leave us a review. This will help us improve and grow as a firm. As a loyal client we want to say thank you in advance.

To make things simple below are a few samples and here is a quick guide to the review process:
Here is a definition of the ranking system:
* We completely let you down
** There were problems w/ our service
*** We could have done better
**** Our services met your expectations
***** You enjoyed working w/ us

Visit one of these two sites:
http://www.ReviewSiteNumber1.com/yourfirm
http://www.ReviewSiteNumber2.com/yourfirm

Again, thank you.
Best Wishes,
Law Firm of LeBret Homer & Rush
http://www.EstatePlanningAttorneyNoWhereUSA.com

Sample Review For Your Reference:
- "The service was polite and they really made a difficult circumstance comfortable. I am so glad we went to Boise Estate Planning attorney Jane Smith..."
- "I have been working with Boise Estate Planning attorney Jane Smith for years and I am glad to have you in my corner and on my side, thanks for always getting done what you promise"
- "At first I was unsure if I needed any firm. After a few visits I am so glad I chose Boise Estate Planning attorney Jane Smith. Not only did I need a firm Jane really made the whole process painless."

```
===================================================================
```

Remember that this isn't all about Google Places / Google + Local; we want to send people to a few different directories. You do of course want reviews going to Google Places / Google + Local as well, but you need to diversify. So have cards with other review sites on them too, such as Yelp, CitySearch, and the others that you've identified in your target directory listings. Try not to put them all on one card, however: it looks cramped, awkward, and unprofessional. A card per review site looks much better, and it'll work better in getting clients to go to the review sites for you.

The same goes for your emails; your clients may already have an account on one of these review sites and then it would be even easier for them to leave a review saying what a wonderful job you did! This also helps even more since identified reviews count even more than anonymous ones!

Again, it's important to note that these are absolutely, positively not testimonials: these are things consumers can go and do on their own. In fact, you're simply trying to encourage a behavior that's already happening: don't be surprised if, when you start this process, you already have a couple of reviews scattered around the Internet. All you're doing is encouraging this process: you're saying "Hey, there are these review sites out there and having reviews help us. You might do it already, and if you liked our service, your review will really help our Internet ranking and get more people into our door!"

You'll find, more often than not, that people are more than willing to help you out in this regard! They'll go to these sites and fill out reviews, and this is super-important: it's one of the driving forces behind the Google Places / Google + Local rankings, and by having this steady system of reviews you're ensuring your steady climb to the top!

SUMMARY:

- Reviews are very important, and should not be overlooked: search the review sites and find out which ones you should be focusing on.

- Make sure you have a system in place to get users to review you: this is different from testimonials!

- Whatever you do, don't have a computer in your office for clients to write reviews (and absolutely don't write their reviews for them). Google requires the reviews to be written by the client on a computer outside of the office, and so the reviews need to be done on the client's own computer!

- Some agencies can Post Reviews for you. Be careful about who you hire to do your review marketing: some marketers will promise huge numbers but write fake reviews with duplicate content and severely damage your Google ranking!

8

USING AUTOMATION TO DO YOUR WORK FOR YOU

Follow-up strategies are a vital segment of any Internet marketing strategy, and it's equally vital that you automate it as much as possible; many businesses will try to do this manually, but the overhead required to manually implement isn't feasible for most businesses. It's vital that you don't spend manual time fielding emails and responding one by one; we've had clients in the past that literally sent out e-mail newsletters every week by hand. If somebody new came in, they'd get manually added to this email list.

That sort of system may work in the beginning, but it's easy to see that it doesn't scale up well at all. You need an automated method of follow-up that both preserves quality but also scales out well, freeing up resources and keeping your Internet marketing strategy running smoothly and efficiently!

Follow-up Framework

First off, we have to talk about the framework for follow-up: when we're talking about follow-up, we're talking about traffic generated to you. We're not talking about people that come in through the door necessarily. We're talking about follow-up that happens when the person finds you. You need a follow-up strategy whether or not the contact is initiated by phone, email, or online via the website.

When a new client gets to your website and chooses to give their name, phone number, and email address, they go into your funnel. Your funnel is the resource you have where you capture your leads and market to them specifically from there. The reason for this is that they've gone through the trouble of giving you this information—they're a "warm lead" and obviously interested, and you have to get to them fast! The whole function of the funnel is to provide you with a resource that enables this sort of rapid response to whatever communication the client happened to initiate.

The best way to do this is to set up an autoresponder system. This system will provide two things to you: it's going to alert you that someone's given you information, and it's going to send them a message immediately. There are a couple of ways to do this, and later on we'll talk about different techniques including texting and direct voicemail. The most traditional and common auto response, however, is an email—that's something they should be getting immediately. A typical auto response email could look something like this:

> Hi Mark,
>
> Somehow not all vanilla ice-cream is created equal. In fact, in my opinion, there are plenty of cartons that shouldn't even be allowed to call themselves vanilla.
>
> Finding the right attorney to help you can be like picking out vanilla ice-cream for the 1st time...
>
> You are not 100% sure you are getting what you need for the situation you have.
>
> Sometimes what you really need is more information before you make any decision.
>
> There is a reason you still have not made any decisions and my report may not have answered all your questions. I find that every situation is a little different and I would almost 100% guarantee that your personal situation is unique and needs answers beyond what you already have.
>
> Of course there are not enough hours in a week for me to talk to everyone with a question, and I wish I could, so I can say that I will be able to connect with you today, but give my office a call and ask for when the next opening is on our firm's calendar.
>
> We can spend 15 minutes on the phone and a lawyer from our firm will personally answer questions you have about elder law and working with attorneys.
>
> Just tell the person that answers that I sent you this email and said it was ok that we scheduled a call this week or next.
>
> We are here to help you with this process. Until we talk to you, have a great day.
>
> All The Best,

That's an example of something they should be getting immediately after they submit their information on your web page. There are many services out there that provide these types of auto responding systems: Constant Contact, AWeber, InfusionSoft, Instant Customer, etc. Whichever service you go with, you have to make absolutely sure that they have a system in place capable of capturing names, storing names in an organized way, and making it as easy and automated as possible to send out those auto responses.

You also need to have a strategy in place for phone numbers. If someone gives you their phone number, you should not only email them right away, but also email someone in your office right away a note that says, "Hey, this person called interested in this. Here's their number." The reason for this is that the Internet is 24 hours; it doesn't close, it's always open, and your website is happily receiving visitors all around the clock. Your office hours, however, are only during the day. If your office hours are nine to five, for example, you won't be answering phones at ten in the evening.

The reason for emailing your office member is that if somebody comes across your website at night and submits their information, they get an immediate email. Then when your office manager gets in the next morning at nine, they can see the email and know someone tried to get in touch. They can then pick up the phone and say, "Hey, this is Jane from Bill's Heating and Air. I saw you downloaded our special report - I hope it helped you out. I'm just calling to ask if there's anything we can help you with."

This is a very personal follow-up to a warm lead, with an emphasis on the personal. We can't stress that enough—you're a local business providing a service to the community and you need to reach out and make those personal connections. An automated email is the minimum touch effort and very easy to do. If they've gone through the trouble of giving you their email, you need to email back saying thanks and share your special report with them. Then email them again a few days later with another message. These should be automated. You can have a few templates for these emails that you can send out to your warm leads.

It's very important to implement an email and phonecall system and use them regularly. This isn't e-commerce, and you're probably not going to close any first time visitors into an online sale. There's no magic shopping cart or impulse buy button that's going to automatically give you a paid customer without any legwork. You are still a local business, and you're engaged in local Internet marketing – but you can't just send out email and expect things to happen. You need to get that phone call or get them to come in to your business in person in order to seal the deal!

Another good best practice is to email out one of your blog posts per month. Just take one of your blog posts each month, any one of them, and send it out to anyone on your email list. It's very easy to send out what's called a "broadcast message" to anyone on your email list that is open to receiving communication from you. The reason you want to do this is that, on the whole, this Internet marketing strategy is a long-term strategy. Your clients may be thinking they need a roofer but they may not need one quite yet. That doesn't mean, however, they won't need one down the line, and these periodic emails will let them remember who you are. This is called "top of mind awareness" in marketing; you want to be the first to come to mind to your warm lead down the road. They may one day think, "Oh! My friend needs info about how to hire a roofer. I've been getting these emails from a business down the road that specializes in roofing. Maybe I'll give them a call and see if they can answer my questions!"

SUMMARY:

- Follow-up is important, but it's equally important that your follow-up process be automated: no one should be sending out newsletters or follow-ups by hand, or adding anyone manually to lists.

- Don't just follow-up with your leads when they fill out a form: follow-up in the office as well. This lets a staff member call the lead as soon as possible, while they're still warm, and shows the lead that you're friendly and ready to do business.

- It's important to keep regular contact with your clients: fire off a blog post once a month to your email lists, in order to keep your business at the top of their minds.

9

ROI AND MAKING MORE THAN YOUR SPENDING

In typical advertising solutions that we've seen from clients, most of the ad dollars get spent in the Yellow Pages, Newspaper and Magazines along with TV and some Radio and Direct Mailers. These make up the vast majority of advertising budgets with clients that we've worked with. They're usually not spending too much money online, and if they are, it's an extension of the Yellow Pages that's usually not well-tracked and often very ineffective.

Advertising online, however, has a huge advantage over traditional advertising methods normally used by most businesses: it's extraordinarily easy to track what's going on throughout the entire online process. You can track pretty well what's happening in each stage of the game: who emailed, what's in the funnel, what's going on, etc. This is very difficult to do with regular advertising; quite often, the only method of communication that traditional advertising media gives a client is a phone number. Unless you're asking them where they heard about you or you're creating a unique phone number for each ad (which is, by the way, a very good best practice; more on that later), you're not getting very good information at all about how your advertising budget is helping you!

In contrast to these traditional advertising methods, you can glean vast amounts of data from the Internet and the tools available to you. You can track how many people visit, and what keywords they typed in that led them to clicking your site. If they visit your Google Places / Google + Local page, you can have instant knowledge there, including who visited, when, and how. Some directory listings have tracking data in place as well;

the big one here, however, is Google Analytics.

Google Analytics is an absolute must-have for your website. If it's not already on your website, ask your webmaster to integrate Google Analytics with your site; if they can't, it's time to find another webmaster. That's how important Google Analytics is to your ROI (Return on Investment). It tells you who's visiting, who's clicking, what data they're entering, how well your website is converting leads, how long your clients stay on your site, and more!

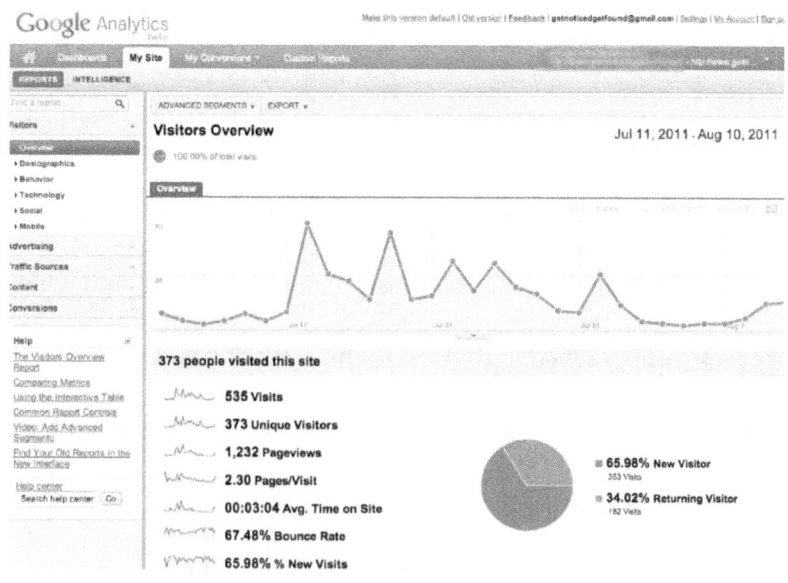

It's an absolutely essential tool for monitoring your ROI and your website, and it needs to be there.

Ok, you're a local businessperson right? Not an online marketing geek. While tracking hits and calls is very important (you do need to know where your money is going), we found that most business owners just don't have the time to do this on a consistent basis. That's why for our private clients, we implemented a system where we track all traffic on their website... and all of the calls to the office. Then at the end of the month, they get a detailed report on all of the action.

We mentioned above having different phone numbers for each ad... even that is more easily tracked online. There are services online that allow you to create different unique forwarding numbers that all forward to your actual number; the only difference is that the call statistics are online and you can quickly see at a glance how many calls each number received. This isn't to say you have to get rid of your current phone number—in fact, you shouldn't. These numbers are only forwarding numbers and nothing more; clients with your old number can still get through perfectly fine.

Another great tool is Google Webmaster Tools, specifically because it tells you how many people are linking to you across the Internet and thus how well your Internet marketing strategy is doing overall. This should be complemented by statistics on your email funnel and autoresponders—you should be able to see how many people are getting / opening your emails and keep track of that as well. On top of all that, there's your own internal CRM (Customer Relationship Management system): how much money you're charging, how long you've been working together, how long you spend with each client, etc. and so forth. As we'll see, that's an incredibly key resource in determining your ROI.

On that note, we're assuming that you already have an internal CRM in place—it is crucial for this process and others. Discussing the process and tools to manage internal CRM is beyond the scope of this book, and there are many resources available to provide you help and support with implementing your own CRM. It's a vital step in the chain, and you need to have one before you can accurately calculate your ROI.

There are an almost unlimited number of things you can track online in order to measure your ROI, and if you're going to take anything away from this section it is this: it's imperative that you have a strong, stable, well-defined system in place in order to correctly track your ROI. Most of the clients we work with believe they have a process in place, but when it's subjected to a rigorous examination it turns out that it breaks down. It's a good step that they even have a system in place—it's good sense and a standard marketing practice. They're spending money, and they want to know where that money's going and how that money's helping them. For an Internet marketing strategy, however, you need to go above and beyond: you need to be taking in the data that show you the point of entry for all your clients.

An example monthly run down might look something like this:

in total, 155 people visited our site this month. Of those visits, 35 came from Google Places / Google + Local, 120 from Google organic search, and 12 from Facebook fan pages. Of these 155 visits, we followed up with all of them; of the clients we followed up with, we closed 45, and each one of them was worth $1200 on average.

This is very basic, and the numbers are simply example numbers, but it should give you an idea of how you should be looking at and tracking your Internet marketing strategy. This allows you to really get an accurate sense of valuation from clients that find you online: Are they worth the same amount as clients who found you driving by, or from referral? We want to make sure you're capturing ROI information from those clients online, and these are extremely important statistics for you to know. Very often, we end up having to build new systems and processes for clients to get this reporting accurate; make absolutely sure that when planning out your overall Internet marketing strategy, you decide what metrics you're going to use and just how you're going to track them!

We can't stress this point enough: it's vital that you have an understanding of your ROI online all the time. Efficient and accurate monitoring in this realm gives you an unparalleled advantage over traditional media; you can know down to the dollar whether spending in the online arena is good for your ROI. In fact, we tell most of our clients that if they're not getting at least three times their ROI on their Internet marketing that something is really wrong. Usually, it's more than that; three times the ROI is our bare minimum for clients to see. If you're not getting that, it means something's wrong and you need to go back and look again at your strategy. Either you've missed something along the way, or you're in a really competitive market and you need to bring in an expert to help you break into the market.

Tracking your own ROI also gives you another advantage: should you choose to hire a marketing agency for your Internet marketing, you can tell whether or not the marketing agency you hired is working well or not, and you can know whether you should stick with them or find someone new.

TIP:

If you're working with an agency, you should absolutely require them to provide you with these ROI reports. You will be required to implement the tracking processes in your business first, and then they should be able to compile the data for you.

Understanding your ROI, understanding your Analytics, using online-only phone numbers; all of these things simply underscore a philosophy that you should always adhere to in your online Internet marketing strategy: use every tool and resource available to you to know where your dollars are going and whether or not your online advertising dollars are really pulling their weight. The more control you have over your information flow and tracking information, the more valuable your online strategy is going to be and, ultimately, the more valuable your business as a whole will become!

SUMMARY:

- ROI tracking on print and TV ads is scarce and ineffectual at best: online ROI tracking offers a wealth of information, and enables you to very precisely track where your money is going and how much of it is coming back.

- It's imperative that you have a strong, stable, well-defined system in place in order to correctly track your ROI. Know where your money is going, know what sites are giving you hits, and know what percentage of leads you're converting, from which sites, and how much you're converting them for - on average at the very least!

- If you work with a marketing agency, it's vital that they give you these ROI reports.

10

WHERE DO I GO FROM HERE

If you've reached this chapter, give yourself a pat on the back: you've done more for your online Internet marketing strategy than many local businesses will ever do. You've got a very, very solid foundation for pulling clients in from the web; you're ranked high with a no-nonsense website that calls to action, you're a Facebook and Twitter regular, and you have in place a sophisticated system of follow-ups and ROI tracking that will enable you to pinpoint your highest-profit channels with incredible accuracy.

That's no reason to get complacent because the Internet is, by its very nature, a fast-moving target. Internet marketing isn't always going to stay the same, and you'll have to work to keep up with it. With that in mind, this chapter is dedicated to what's coming up down the road: things that you should be very interested in pursuing as well. These are things that a local business has to think about. New technologies and trends that will have to be incorporated into your marketing strategy in order to keep at the top of your game!

Mobile

We've held this particular topic to the very end, but this is perhaps the most immediate of all the coming challenges for Internet marketing. Mobile devices are rapidly becoming the primary mode of interaction with the Internet; Mary Meeker of Morgan-Stanley has recently estimated that, given current mobile trends, the number of mobile devices that connect to the Internet eclipses that of regular desktop PCs. You heard that right: in 2014, more people will be connecting to the Internet by phone than by computer.

In fact, mobile is already a driving force behind many of the search engine changes we've seen. Google is setting up its local places infrastructure because it believes information is going mobile. Mobile search is a different creature than traditional search; it's more often an immediate need. Users who search mobile are typically driven by an "I need something right now that's near me" mentality, as opposed to a more research-oriented desktop user who's more willing to sift through answers and Wikipedia articles. Very few people will be doing that on a mobile phone; most likely they're looking for a business nearby they can walk or drive to quickly.

This is great news, even for professionals, although many professionals have looked skeptically at us when we've said this. Very often, people are out at lunch, driving around, or talking about stuff and think of their problem. More and more, they'll just think to themselves "Oh! I'll just use my phone really quick and search for an answer". The same applies to sitting around eating dinner or watching TV; chances are they have their iPhone, Android phone, or tablet sitting right next to them. Instead of waiting and looking up the answer to their problem later, they'll just pick up their mobile device and look up the answer right then and there.

This might seem far-fetched, but it's actually not: think about your own mobile smartphone use, or the usage patterns you've observed in others. There's a clear aura of instant gratification with any sort of mobile device, and users take advantage of it and get an instant answer. If your site's not mobile-friendly or your Google Places / Google + Local page is non-existent (Google Places / Google + Local is extremely mobile friendly) you're going to get left out in the cold!

The mobile realm also tightens up the ranking requirements quite a bit. On the regular desktop Internet, you've got to be in the top 7 ranking; it'd be nice to be in the top 3 or 4, but 7's the bare minimum. On mobile devices, if you're not top 2 you're not being seen; very few people scroll down on mobile phones, and often they simply tap the first or second result they see.

This is important to you because mobile phones offer an unparalleled ease of use. For example, many phones like iPhone and Android offer built-in calling from the web. Users can simply tap a finger on your phone number and the smartphone dials the number automatically, without any need to ever pick up another phone. As mobile devices are more and more common, it's of critical importance that your site is mobile-friendly and sits in that A or B listing on Google's result returns!

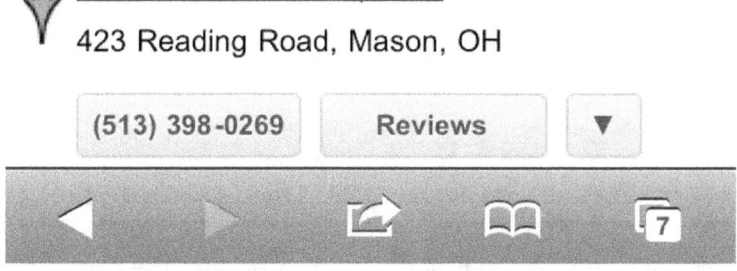

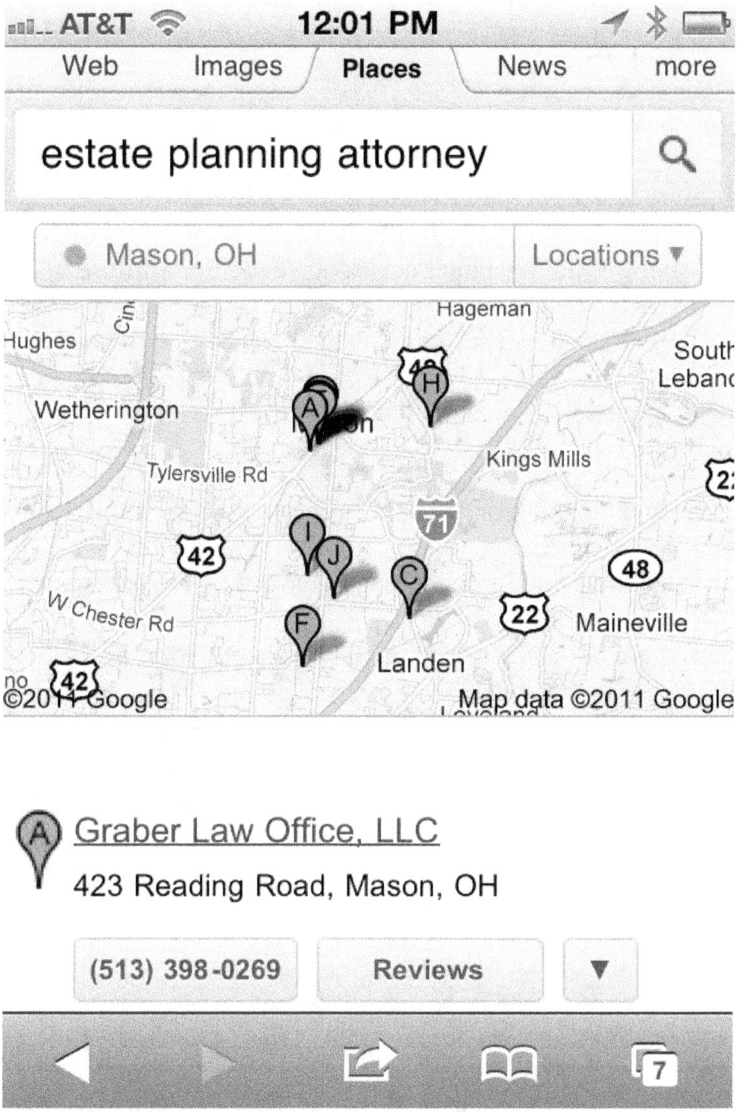
AT&T
12:01 PM
Web
Images
Places
News
more
estate planning attorney
Mason, OH
Locations
Hageman
Hughes
Wetherington
Tylersville Rd
Kings Mills
42
71
48
22
W Chester Rd
Maineville
Landen
©2011 Google
Map data ©2011 Google
Graber Law Office, LLC
423 Reading Road, Mason, OH
(513) 398-0269
Reviews
7

Social

We've obviously covered a great deal of social media previously, and you're well-equipped to handle the social network scene at the moment. What we didn't cover, however, is the future of social networks - how they're going to change and how that's going to impact your overall online marketing strategy.

The first and most important aspect of future social is this: eventually, social media services are going to be more than just places where people connect. Social media networks are transforming into something more search engine oriented; people will go to Facebook not just to interact, but to search for things as well. This makes it crucial that you have an established presence early on.

It's not too late, and you are not behind the curve: just make sure you start now establishing presences on sites like LinkedIn, Twitter, Facebook, YouTube, StumbleUpon, Digg, and other social media sites. This doesn't mean you have to interact with all of these social media network every day or even frequently -

though you're going to want to keep more in touch with the big ones as we covered in the social network chapter. What you do want, however, is a presence. Just make sure that your listings are in fact on these websites - you'll be very glad for it later!

Social networks are also getting very location-oriented as time goes on, so we can expect that trend to continue: this will eventually lead to a sort of social-mobile combo: users who are Google searching while also in their Facebook mobile app. This is already a user pattern that exists, and we've noticed a rise in this user behavior recently; it's actually quite common now. Users are in the Facebook app and just go to the places listing and see what's around them. The first reaction is that this makes the most sense for restaurants and bars, and they've already start to capitalize on that. But this is useful for businesses as well: users will note "oh, this is where so-and-so office is" and they'll remember it. You need to have this local presence, because if you're not there and you're not found, someone else will be!

This social / search hybrid that we're seeing slowly creep up is also forming another important piece of Internet marketing: a combination of social word-of-mouth and Google ranking. Instead of letting Google figure out who's first, more people are going to go on Facebook and see what their friends think. Your interaction level, reviews, and presence on Facebook are going to be crucial at this stage of the game: more people are going to search there the way they're currently searching on Google. Some Internet results will still trickle through, but for the most part the results will come from the client's social networks.

This is important because people in general will take how their friends and family have viewed businesses very, very seriously. From a marketing perspective, it's a long-known and oft-proven fact that people give far more weight to opinions from friends and family than from any other source of marketing. As a result, this combo of social is search is going to be very influential, and you should stay on top of it as it progresses.

Direct Mailing To Online Source

You may wonder why we're putting direct mailing in the "What's Next" category. In Internet marketing terms, direct mailing is older than dust. The reason it's here is that there's definite potential for it as the years roll on. Like fashion from decades gone by coming back around and becoming popular again, direct mailing is making a comeback. The reason for this is partly because of its scarcity. Receiving mail every now and then, done properly, is not a poor marketing option. It's not something you should rely on heavily, but it's definitely something to keep in your arsenal and use where it's appropriate.

If you already have a direct mail campaign going and want to keep doing it, you need to find a way to incorporate Google Places / Google + Local, Facebook, your website, or a call to action in your direct mailers; you have to shift the goal to getting people online. Direct mailing with mobile is an especially attractive option; being able to snap a picture and go straight to a website to see info or reviews or being able to text a certain number to get a special report are options that look very promising.

Texting

As mentioned with direct mailing, you can now have people text a number to receive information; they're actually entering your marketing funnel the moment they text that number. This is all automatic, too; you can have the same autoresponder system set up so that it sends texts in the same way that it sends emails. If a user puts in their mobile phone number, they get a text that says something like "We've received your name and email. Thank you very much for getting in contact! Check your email for a special report, free of charge. One of our representatives will be in touch!"

There is one other aspect about texting that should be mentioned here: some in the restaurant / bar type business have automatic texts that send the latest coupons or deals - Tuesday happy hours, Five for Four Fridays, marketing promotions like that. It's very common in the restaurant / bar scene, and we're implementing those some ideas with our local business owners. Make sure to contact us at: info@123MarketingResults.com and stay up-to-date with our research in this area!

Once they give out their mobile phone number, don't be afraid to send out texts once or twice a month. Make sure the texts are useful, and don't send them more than once or twice per month; that could start to feel 'spammy' for them. Texts are read over 90% of the time once received as opposed to emails, which are read only 17-20% of the time (and those are optimistic numbers). A well-placed, well-timed text or two every now and then can really help drum up some business and get some clients to call you!

Direct Voicemail

Direct voicemail is the practice of sending a voicemail directly to the phone without the phone ever ringing; this is possible to do now with mobile phone voicemail systems, and in actuality it works very well. These systems are quite nifty; you can set up outbound voicemails that talk about something new or something local that you and your business did. The voicemail can be about thirty to ninety seconds, and instead of calling you can send it directly to their phone. The voicemail notifier pops up but the phone never rings, meaning the client can see the voicemail message and listen whenever they want. It's non-intrusive and as a result the listen rate is much higher.

This is one of the reasons we recommended earlier to get mobile phone numbers from your leads; it not only opens up the texting avenue but the direct voicemail avenue as well. The direct voicemail is very personal and very effective, and its best used for getting the word out about your local events or sharing interesting things your business might be doing. An example might be seminars - if your business does educational events, dropping a direct voicemail to each of your customers is a great, personal way to let them know about your upcoming seminars. It's easy, non-intrusive, and works very well!

NOTE:

We called this chapter the "What's Next" chapter for a reason; many of these technologies are already beginning to affect the Internet marketing arena. We've begun to implement these things with some of our clients who are ahead of the curve or are battling in very competitive markets, which illustrates that these ideas are not simply theory or fluff. They're real strategies that are in the market now, and it's a good idea to look into them now, because if you don't your competitors are!

Talk to an agency that you're working with and see what their ideas are on these new strategies. Nothing's set in stone with them, and a creative idea or two could really put you ahead in these arenas. It's also important that you find the right agency, one who specializes in these techniques; these aren't things your average webmaster will know how to do, and chances are an average webmaster hasn't even heard of them! Make sure you talk to an agency or service that thoroughly understands the full realm of Internet marketing, how it works with other marketing, and knowledge of future strategies down the line.

For more, be sure to visit our website www.123MarketingResults.com

SUMMARY:

- Mobile and social media are going to be the driving forces in marketing over the next few years: both are driving marketing to be more location-oriented, due to the always-on nature that combines and unites mobile and social. Keep up to date on them and don't miss any opportunities to be creative and capitalize on these markets!

- People give much stronger weight to opinions from friends:

make sure you have a strong social presence, and leverage that social presence by having a well-established business that will rank high in the inevitable search / social hybrid arena.

- Direct mailing still has a place in the world, but it should be driving clients to go to your website in order to get that warm lead and—more importantly—get them to use a channel that's more easily tracked and analyzed.

- Don't ever be complacent: always think of new ways to innovate and incorporate new technologies, and make sure to work with agencies who have a good feel for the online field, are specialists in the online marketing world, keep up to date on the trends, and know how to help you stay at the top of your game.

11

HOW TO GET ALL OF THIS DONE AND HOW TO FIND PEOPLE TO DO THIS FOR YOU

The last thing you're going to need is a workforce. Let's face it, you didn't build your business just so you could spend 11 hours a day uploading videos, submitting listings to directories, and designing websites.

Now we really wish we had better news for you, but finding competent people in the Phoenix area to do this work for you is not easy. Most web designers are broke, they know nothing about marketing, and many don't have any clients outside of your local city, and yes, they often live in their parent's spare room. This is not the kind of person you can trust with your marketing budget, so be thorough in deciding who to invest with.

We get asked all the time where to find a good web person. And our answer is that every time we find one who knows what they are doing (they are rare), we hire them to work on our team!

Outsourcing this work to overseas or to some fly-by-night business will cause more work than it will save. You'll generally find that was work was not done properly and often times will be required to be re-done.

And having one of your assistants or a family member do this work will drive you both crazy and possibly irreversibly ruin your relationship.

So How Can I Get All Of This Done?

First, by now you'll agree, local web marketing is probably the most time-sensitive, urgent issue on your calendar right now. It doesn't seem like it at the moment, but when you look back on this book six to eighteen months from now, you will probably wish that you had a time machine to get you back to this day.

The local Internet marketing door is still open right now, but it is closing fast... and we would not want you to miss out on securing the financial future of your business just because you had no time.

On the other hand, it's very difficult to find good people to help you with your online presence. Most web designers are flakes. And even if they knew how to put up a good site, it doesn't mean they can get you on page #1 of Google multiple times. And outsourcing this kind of work to a country where English is not the primary language - or to a friend or relative - is a waste of time and money.

We would love to offer the services of our marketing agency, but at the time of this writing, we are almost full with our current Phoenix area business clients... and our commitment is to them.

In the interest of full disclosure, we provide a turn-key, 100% Done-For-You service, which means you give us some basic information about your business, and we do the rest. It's literally ALL done for you. Plus, we know how to get results faster than anyone. Our services are not the least expensive, and you will probably be able to find someone to do a bare-bones job for less. But the way to look at it is: we invest a lot of time and money into our client's future. And, when you get 3, 5, or 9 more clients a month at $5,000.00 or more, we all win.

But we're restricting ourselves to only a handful of clients within each business specialty category and geographical area in metropolitan Phoenix. Your business type in your specific location may already be spoken for... and while that's not to say we won't take you, there's a good chance we may be committed already and have to pass.

BONUS!

Having said all of that, if you feel that you are a business that we should choose to work with and you would like to find out about our team's availability to help you and to get all of this DONE FOR YOU, we would like to offer you a BONUS for making it through our book. Simply mention this book and receive your $200 value "Speed to Market Strategy Session" with our compliments.

Contact us at:

Phone: 480-382-3711
Email: info@123MarketingResults.com
www.123MarketingResults.com/Coupon

We will, at the very least, be able to tell you if we are already working with a professional in your same category in your area.

Provided we have a possible opening, we'll start with a "Speed to Market Strategy Session" with one of our consultants. There is no obligation for this complimentary consultation. This just begins the discussion as to how we may be able to help you.

And while we know that some people take this experience-backed, high-quality web strategy then go and hire a cheap local service, we also know that the best customers, those who understand the value of growing their business by maximizing their online marketing investment will ask us to just "do it for me." We are accepting a small number of clients to build a long-term relationship with. And if that sounds like your business, then please feel free to email, text, or call.

With that, you've reached the end of this book, but you certainly haven't reached the end of how we can assist you. If you've followed all the techniques and processes in this book and really took it to heart, you're very prepared to wade into the online marketing arena and come out the victor; you're ahead of most of your competitors and you have a clear idea of what lies in store. Don't get complacent, be creative, and you'll be successful in the online marketing arena for many years to come!

GLOSSARY of TERMS

ANALYTICS: Analytics are technical measures you can take to see what happens with visitors on your website: how long they stay, what they click, how many of them return to the website, and statistics of that nature. One of the best analytic software packages out there currently is Google Analytics, which is also free.

AUTORESPONDER: An autoresponder is a system put in place to automatically respond to communication initiated by a potential client, usually via email. Autoresponders can range from simple to extremely complex, and can either send just one generic email or choose from dozens of templates depending on the form used by the potential client or the information provided to the autoresponder by the potential client.

BING: A major search engine, like Google and Yahoo. It has many of the same features and has the next-largest market share of any of the search engines, after Google.

BLOG: Originally an abbreviation of the term "web log", it has now come to mean a type of website (or part of a website) that is frequently updated with new content and has many interactive options for users to leave comments and otherwise participate; many blogs are powered by software explicitly designed to make this frequent updating an easier and smoother process, like Wordpress or Typepad.

CALL TO ACTION: Content on a website or other method of communication that appeals to the reader to contact the business.

CRM: An acronym for "Customer Relationship Management". In the context of Internet marketing, it most often refers to the software put in place that manages clients and potential clients of the business; names, locations, likes, dislikes, needs, and other information that the business may find relevant.

DIRECTORY: In the sense of Internet marketing, a website or part of a website whose purpose is to list businesses. Many of these, like Yelp, Merchant Circle, or CitySearch, also contain reviews of businesses that are often user-generated and submitted.

DUPLICATE CONTENT: Identical content that appears on multiple websites. Search engines have created ways of detecting this and often have algorithms that even detect if the content has just been altered slightly; content that has just be altered slightly and is still virtually identical to the original content will still be flagged as duplicate content by many search engines.

E-COMMERCE: The buying and selling of products and services over the Internet.

FACEBOOK: A social networking site that is currently the most popular in the world; it allows users to network with each other and socialize, including sharing photos, thoughts, status updates, and wall posts with each other.

FACEBOOK PLACES: A specific segment of the social networking site Facebook that allows users to see local spots around them as well as update their location in real-time from mobile phones or other means, allowing other users to see where they are at any given time.

GEOLOCATION: In Internet marketing and SEO, a term used to describe location-specific information; normally city and state for most local businesses.

GOOGLE MAPS: A part of Google's website that primarily deals with maps and navigation. One of the features of Google Maps is the ability for local businesses to list themselves on it, and the local search return feature was originally a part of this system. Google later integrated it into the main search system when it proved to be popular.

GOOGLE PLACES / GOOGLE + LOCAL: A part of Google's website that allows a business to have a specific page dedicated to them. It often hooks in with their location on Google Maps, and it features user-generated reviews of the business as well as links to other directories and review sites.

IFRAME: Stands for an Inline Frame and is basically an HTML document embedded inside another HTML document on a website. An iFrame pulls the content from one website into another. So in the context of Facebook, an iFrame pulls the content of another website into an area on your Facebook page. iFrames are very powerful because anything you can create on a website, you can bring into your Facebook page, providing a unique and rich experience for your community.

IP ADDRESS: A unique number that identifies a computer on a network.

KEYWORD: A term that a user searches against in a search engine to retrieve content that contains or is relevant to the term.

KEYWORD DENSITY: The use of a specific keyword present in any given piece of content. For example, given the keyword "racing" used five times in a 500-word blog post, the keyword density of "racing" would be 1%. Optimal keyword density is between 3 and 4%, and should not exceed 4% or it may be flagged as spamming.

KEYWORD PHRASE / LONG TAIL KEYWORD PHRASE: A phrase comprised of individual words but treated like a single keyword for the purposes of a search, like "Nascar car racing" or "racing opportunities in Texas".

KEYWORD RICH: Content that has many keywords and uses them often, with good keyword density.

KEYWORD TOOL: Tools created to help select optimal keywords for search engine marketing, like Google's Keyword Tool. They often contain information such as amount of searches for a particular keyword and other metrics that help ascertain how popular or prevalent a given keyword or keyword phrase may be.

LINKEDIN: A social networking site that is geared towards businesses and professionals, enabling them to link up and network more effectively.

LOCAL SEARCH RETURN: A feature within Google's search engine that returns location-specific results for a user who types in keywords that relate to local businesses. For example, a local search return would appear for a user in Omaha, Nebraska who typed in "Cosmetic Dentist" A map and local businesses that are relevant to the search result would appear in the ensuing search page.

NICHING: The practice of specializing your marketing strategy to a certain keyword or keyword phrase in order to rank in the highest spot in a local search return for that keyword or keyword phrase.

ROI: An acronym for "Return on Investment," which means the amount of profit; in literal terms, the amount of money returned for the amount of money invested.

SEARCH ALGORITHM: A series of computer algorithms used by major search engines to index, search, and rank websites on the Internet.

SEARCH ENGINE: A website or company, like Google, Bing, or Yahoo, that indexes other websites on the Internet and allows users to enter keywords in order to find relevant websites.

SEO: An acronym for "Search Engine Optimization." It refers to the section of marketing that tries to increase exposure and clientele by using techniques and strategies to rank high on Internet search engines. Often interchanged with SEM (Search Engine Marketing).

SOCIAL MEDIA: Sites whose primary purpose is to enable users to share content with each other and socialize on the Internet;

examples of websites that fall into this category are Facebook, Twitter, and LinkedIn.

SPAM: In Internet parlance, spam was originally used to refer to any unsolicited bulk messages sent over email. It is now also commonly used to refer to content on the Internet which is not useful and designed to make a page rank higher on search engines by tricking search engine algorithms into rating the content as more useful than it actually is.

TWEET: An individual post on Twitter.

TWITTER: A social networking service that allows users to post 140-character tweets to their account, with the ability for other users to follow them and respond to the tweets.

UNIQUE SELLING POSITION (USP): Unique Selling Position separates you from your competition in a specific market place. The term is often used to refer to any aspect of an object that differentiates it from similar objects.

URL: An acronym for "Uniform Resource Locator". It is the name that the user types into the browser bar in order to access a specific website; for example, "www.google.com" or "www.bing.com" would be examples of URLs

ABOUT THE AUTHORS

Marlene Allen

Business Consultant and Trainer has provided cutting edge new media strategies to businesses in the Phoenix Valley for over 20 years.

Local Business Owner of Marketing Agency: New Media Online Marketing Corporation.
Providing Internet Marketing, Video Marketing, Mobile Marketing, Email Marketing, Customer Relationships and Reputation Marketing including Customer Follow Up and Retention Strategies
Author of the book "Transforming Authors", and co-author of "Online Customers! A How to Guide for Phoenix Business Owners", ghostwriter for several Valley authors.

ABOUT THE AUTHORS

Valerie Dawson

Internet Marketer and Efficiency Expert.

Created over 10 Digital Information Products that have sold in over 20 countries online

Founder of "The Dawson Method" that assists Business Owners to Remove Blocks that may be holding them back in Sales and Growth.

Author of "The Magnetic Mindset" and co-author of "Online Customers! A How to Guide for Phoenix Business Owners."

BRING US TO SPEAK AT YOUR NEXT EVENT:

Want to bring one of the authors to speak at your event?

Our programs are designed to optimize a medical professionals online marketing strategies. Our agency focuses on advanced SEO (Search Engine Optimization) and Local Search as an alternative means to traditional marketing.

Inquire How You Can Book Us To Speak For FREE!

Every year we are subsidized us to speak to a limited number of groups and associations at no cost to them. To inquire about having us speak at your event for no additional charge contact us at: info@123MarketingResults.com or 602-492-5620.

QUANTITY DISCOUNTS

Our books are found on Amazon.

If you would you like to offer this book at your next event or association meeting, we offer quantity discounts. For more information please contact: info@123MarketingResults.com or 602-492-5620.

BONUS!

Discover Exactly How You Can Make a Few Slight Adjustments and Begin to Dominate Local Search… It All Starts with Your "Speed to Market Strategy Session".

www.123MarketingResults.com/coupon

If you want our valuable "Speed to Market Strategy Session" visit this link. There is no obligation of course! This just begins the discussion as to how we may be able to help you. This URL gives you a coupon that makes this $200 review free for you, since you are reading and implementing the things in this book. Note, while it's free, we're busy, and availability may be limited. It's a great opportunity to get your online presence reviewed by one of our experts.

And while we know that some people take this experience-backed, high-quality web strategy then go and hire a cheap local marketing agency, we also know that the best customers, those who understand the value of growing their business by maximizing their online marketing investment will ask us to just "do it for me." We accept high quality clients to build a long-term relationship with. And if that sounds like your business, then please feel free to write or call.

Phone: 602-492-5620

Email: info@123MarketingResults.com

www.ingramcontent.com/pod-product-compliance
Lightning Source LLC
Chambersburg PA
CBHW051650170526
45167CB00001B/399